Coming Through the Flames
My Life in the F.D.N.Y.

By Chris Edwards
With Linda Cotter-Lucas

1

A Note from the Author, Chris Edwards

To all of you, my friends, brothers, family and new friends who will read this book. If you know me, you know how much I loved being a New York City firefighter. When the job retired me, I felt I had unfinished business. I know my younger children and grandchildren never knew daddy/grandpa as a F.D.N.Y. Firefighter. They never saw me in my uniform, so I decided to write notes to let them know what it was like to work in the greatest fire department in the world, and to work with the bravest firefighters in the world; men I will call *my brothers* forever. When I started to write, a friend of mine Linda Cotter-Lucas, who had experience helping people write books, gave me the encouragement to finish. She placed the sentences into paragraphs and paragraphs into chapters. She said that this is a story, not just for your children to remember you by, but for others who have had problems in their lives that they might learn from this book about never giving up! They might learn to always keep moving forward no matter what life throws at you! The book is based on my life growing up as a young man struggling to make ends meet and raise a family, finding a job, then struggling to find out just where I belong in this crazy thing called life. The battles, the losses, the good times and the bad, all along never really seeing the good through all these difficult times. How things on the job would change my life forever, forcing me to take off my blinders and to see what was happening all around me. Not just what was in front of my eyes, but also things I used to overlook. I notice the effect of losing loved ones in my life and the brothers that lost their lives before September 11, 2001 as well as the brothers who lost their lives on that terrible day, and the others who have died since. My life has changed for the better. I have taken my blinders off and see what this crazy life is about, and notice the signs that are sent my way. Through the tears, laughs and the hugs, I was blessed working at the greatest job, a teacher of life's ups and downs, the F.D.N.Y. I've *Come Through the Flames*. I hope my journey can help anyone reading this. A portion of the royalties of this book will go to help firefighters and their families struggling with the unpredictable nature of life and the job.

Chapter Selection

Introduction

I'm so glad to be able to talk to you and share my story. I find that certain events I've gone through have prepared me to handle future stages in my life. Of course, while they were happening I had no idea, but it seems like I embrace things with a sense of wonderment that I've never had before. It's like the blinders are off and I can see why certain events led to others and what they were preparing me for. I still do not know all the answers for everything that has happened to me and my loved ones, but I know if I keep an open mind it will all work out. I know that you understand which is why I'm so comfortable telling you my story. As I sit on top of this mountain, I've been wondering how I got here not physically but mentally and spiritually. I think all my experiences have been opportunities for real growth.

1

The Roast?

You see it started about 29 years ago when I became a firefighter with the fire department of New York, FDNY as it is proudly known. I never thought of becoming a firefighter until I had to find a career and fast! I was married at the age of eighteen and had two children by the time I was twenty. I had taken all the civil service tests that I knew existed. Finally, the FDNY called me! Not knowing what the job was about besides putting water on a fire; I discovered the job really grew on me! I will never forget the first job I had. It was back in 1985. It seems like ages ago. Well, that's because it was! We had a fire in a basement apartment and when we pulled up there was a radio call for children trapped inside. They were screaming for help for what seemed like hours but was only minutes. The truck companies tried in vain to open the apartment door, but they could not cut the steel gates in time, so the two children died a fiery death. I remember my officer and other firefighters who would later be called my brothers, say, "Hey Probie, do you want to go down and bag the roast?" *Roast*, I thought to myself. What a cold way to speak about two young children's death! Well, I thought about it and said to the lieutenant, "If I have to I will, but if I don't, I would rather not. I have a long career ahead of me, and I think I will be bagging bodies and seeing death for a long time." I tried to figure out just why these senior men, the brothers, used the word "roast" to describe the death of two innocent children. Well, later on I realized why. When I got home from work, I went right upstairs to my children's bedroom and hugged them till I cried! This is where it all started.

As we left the job (fire), I said a silent prayer for those two children. When we got back to the quarters, the brothers started breaking balls about not wanting to see the two children (Roasts). All I kept thinking to myself is, *"How can they deal with death this way? Especially the death of young children! Did they have to keep so far from reality, so it didn't eat at their soul?"* I knew right then and there that this job was going to have its ups and downs, its good times and bad times, and its sad times. When I first got the job, I quickly became aware how important it was to know exactly what to do at a fire. There are five firefighters and an officer. The truck has positions for every man. The firefighter with the least time gets the worst position that would be the *canman*. The second man would be the *irons man*. The third spot would be the outside *vent man*. The most senior man would have the roof. What I realized was I love the action of being on the inside... nearer to the fire. Even after a couple of years, I would still love to get close to the fire and battle it. You see the fire has a life of its own; it dances, it rolls, it bounces around the room. It rolls like waves in the ocean on the shore, but when you

11

feed it oxygen, it becomes deadly. The firehouse I worked in back in the late 80's was in the top 20 truck companies in the city. It was too slow for me. I would work all of the 4th of July's because that was one of the busiest days. You might end up with three or four fires a night. I notice certain brothers at the firehouse always worked that day. I quickly figured out that if you want to see fires, work on the 4th of July or the days before and after...

2

The Brotherhood

As the years went by I realized that there would be things you have control of and others you just left in God's hands and prayed for the best, both on and off the job. My personal life was in constant turmoil between relationships, family, and financial problems. You see someone told me years ago you will never be rich as a New York City Firefighter. You always have to have two or three jobs. That's just the way it was going to be! Well mixed with the money not being great and trying to raise two children, and then four children, it made things both in and out of the firehouse difficult. Unfortunately when you work a second job, you get tired which puts everyone at a risk. Brothers would sit at the kitchen table working out their schedules for the next week. Some guys would work weekends, and others would have special days they needed off. Some would juggle their shifts around their wife's work schedules. It was crazy! When we got new firefighters they were called *Probies.* I would tell them the fire department and this firehouse is their number one job! The day the firehouse becomes your second job is the day you can get seriously hurt!

Now the great thing besides fighting fires was the relationship you made with guys you worked with. If there was something you needed like a project you wanted help with, all you had to do was write it on the board, and there would be 50 brothers coming to your house to help! Everyone had a specialty in one thing or another. It was great! These are the guys you could count on both in and outside the firehouse. These were the guys you laughed with, fought with, and cried with. You shared breakfast, lunch, dinner, family events, weddings, kid's birthdays, holidays, funerals, fishing trips, canoe trips, parties, and boys' night out. These were the brothers you would lay your life on the line for and know they would be there for you no matter what! The time we shared at the kitchen table was priceless. The moment you walked in the door to start your tour, they would be joking and ragging on you. They had an old saying which said, "When they bust your chops, laugh because if they see it bothered you they would never give up on it!" So when I started the job, I laughed all the time no matter what they said about me. It drove the senior guys crazy that I laughed all the time and didn't get mad. Then, about 20 years later I ran into a retired senior man who greeted me with a hug and said, "Edwards you haven't stopped laughing all these years!" At that moment, I realized I got them! LOL!

You see it's when they bust your balls, you take it. It's when they don't say anything to you that you know you have a problem like you are a square rooter (someone who only thinks of himself), and the job has them. You can tell from the minute a brother or probie walks through the back door if he is a lifer or a ¾ guy. A ¾ guy is a guy who is looking to find a way out before he even starts the job. That's the guy you have to watch because he is the one who will get you hurt. He's not a student of the job. He wants to get out as soon as the opportunity arises. We call brothers like that *square rooters, hairbags.* There is a sign made for them, and it is one-way!   That's when the trouble starts!

3

Code 10-45 Code 1

As time went by, I realized that everyone handled death in different ways. Some guys drank, others guy became very cold about death. I would pray silently to myself for the "Code 10-45 code 1"... which is a person who died at a job (the Roast). I remember we were relocated to another firehouse to cover their area. During the fire, we heard that there was a "10-45 code 1" in the area. After a couple of hours, the dispatcher told us to return to our firehouse. On the way back, the dispatcher said, "L46 head over to the job (fire)" By now the fire was under control. The dispatcher asked the officer, "Do you have any body bags?" When the officer turned and questioned us about having body bags, I noticed we only had salvage

17

plastic sheets which we use to cover windows after fires. Now we head over to the fire on 3rd Ave in the Bronx, and the officer tells the chief we only have salvage plastic. The chief said there was a code 10-45 code 1, so the officer and I went up to see the dead person. It was a two-story taxpayer with steep stairs leading to the second floor. As we got up to the 2nd floor, we saw the building's whole roof was gone, and the victim was lying in the middle of the floor. He was burnt beyond recognition. Only his head was facing the far wall and his feet towards the stairs. They also said they heard him screaming for help for about 10 minutes and the brothers couldn't reach him. He had pants on, and the pants were open to tell us what sex the victim was. He had a pair of sneakers and no shirt on. He was burnt to the point that his skin was black. As the officer walked away, I said a prayer for the man. Not knowing if he was a rich, poor, good or bad or if he had a family, I just prayed for his soul.

At this point, we have a probie working that night who brought the salvage sheets up the stairs. I knew the dead man had sneakers on, and no shirt and his head and shoulders were exposed. We lay out the plastic next to him. I knew this was going to be a mess when we had to roll his body onto the plastic. The probie had to grab the victim's shoulders, and I had to grab the feet with the sneakers and pants on. He goes to grab him, and the body slips off his hands and all the skin comes off the body! The probie gags!! That was the distraction I needed to get my mind off what we had to do. We proceeded to try and lift the body as he complained that he could not grab anything to lift him. I said... one, two, and three lift!! We lifted the body, and he put him on the plastic, but his gloves and sleeves were full of the man's burnt skin. The probie gags again. It gives me relief and distraction for a moment before we do what we had to do. We wrapped the 10-45 in the plastic and started heading for the stairs. I turn the feet around, so the man's head is facing the stairs. I knew the man's head would be facing the probie, but I didn't realize the victim's head would keep banging up against the probie's chest the whole way down the stairs causing the probie to gag all the way

19

down. It caused me further distraction enough to keep my mind off of what was really happening. We got the body down the stairs and onto the sidewalk where the probie began to get sick and vomit. Again looking at the probie, it took my mind off of this poor soul who screamed for 10 minutes in hell. Other firefighters came over, and we started busting on the probie. *"Hey kid what's for dinner "roast beef"! "Hey, I like my steak medium rare!!"* The probie removed his turnout coat covered in black burnt skin and gagged all the way back to quarters. We joked about the victim's private part size and the probie having the man's head banging on his chest. I realized I was doing the same thing that the old timers did to me with the first 10-45 and how I couldn't bare looking at the victim. As time went on I would drive back to that building that is leveled and hold on to my rosary beads and pray for that ***"10-45 code 1."*** ....

4

Walk In Our Boots

I started to realize that there were some friends who I knew were working with the NYPD that had no respect for the Fire Dept. I would have friends say, "How much sleep did you get last night?" I realized that they were jealous of the job that I loved. Some of them tried to get on the list, but either they didn't pass the physical, or they got a bad grade on the written. I would let a lot of it slide, but then there were others that got me mad! This was all before September 11, 2001, and soon after which made me pissed!! For the people and friends that had something to say before 9-11, I felt I had to defend the greatest job in the world. You see people had an image of what the job was, but that was either from a friend or a TV show. They never saw what happened behind the scenes of a 24-hour tour in a New York City Firehouse. They would say, "All you firefighters do is sleep and eat." So I would turn their words back on them and ask them how many shootouts they were involved in? Some of them worked in good neighborhoods in the city just like the fire department. If you wanted to work, you had to go to bad neighborhoods overrun with crime and drugs. The fires followed those areas. Some of the cops I had respect for; others I would argue with. You see, in bad neighborhoods, the cops have no safe place to stay but the local firehouse. They would put a couple of fresh-faced rookies on the corner right in the middle of the dealers just to stir up the bee hives. These poor guys would ask to come in and take a break. You see we all have the same cause in mind and the same goal of keeping the good people of the city safe.

Now, I have a cousin who works as a college professor along with her husband. She never said anything, but her husband always would have something to say about money. I remember him doing it to my father as a kid growing up. My father was one of the first NYC Sanitation Cops. When my cousin would visit, he would start with my father, he would say, *"So Charlie how much money did you scam from the store owners today?" I know you have to be making money on the side."* My father would come back and say, *"Hey David, why don't you teach your students the truth about our country instead of all your communist bullshit!!"* This would go back and forth with my father shutting him up after a while. I didn't understand till my father passed away how hard a job my father had compared to the piece of cake job Dave had. I also didn't realize the amount of money Dave made compared to my father's salary until I got older. You see where he left off with my father, he started in with me about the FDNY. When he came to visit, I was always ready to hear it. He would start with *" So Chris how much sleep did you get last night or how much TV did you watch and what are you doing with all the money you make?"* This was something that drove me crazy. (Remember in the firehouse always laugh when they think they bother you) With Dave, I didn't care, I would come right back at him with the same venom as he came after my father and me. Then one night while working in E75, we had a run late at night for an order of smoke. The fire was so bad, and a brother died that night!! (A firefighter died right in front of us) I was hurt; I had a broken finger while searching for him and I didn't want to get the finger fixed. I felt, *"A firefighter just died, and I am going to the hospital for a finger?"* A brother is dead!! Well to stay after the funeral and see his widow and young children made me cry my eyes out for them, but I couldn't wait to see Dave!!! ... to be continued...

5

The Unforgiving Red Devil

Now I must explain to you about the job I had
with the broken finger where I needed to tap
out but had to see the job through. It was a pull
box on the corner of East Fordham Road. I was
on a detail (when a firehouse is short they take
a firefighter from one house and bring him to
theirs to make it full strength). The call came in
at 1 am. The pull box was on the corner. We got
off the rig (firetruck), and it was a two-story
taxpayer. There were a mattress store, an
eyeglass shop, and a clothing store that ran
above the two other stories. The truck looked
through the window of the mattress store, and I
saw a light haze, and when they took the roll

down gate to the eyeglass shop, and the truckie went in to do the search. We had the line to the eyeglass place and started to push the line in. There were high ceilings, and it was a deep store. We started to move forward when all of a sudden you could see the thick dark smoke rolling over our heads. It looked like waves rolling above our head on a beach during the summertime. Then, all of a sudden that dark smoke found some air and started to light up! All hell broke loose! The truckies (the guys who go in without water) were so far in the back that they had to bail out!   They ran right over us and out the door. We were more than halfway to the back of the store, and it lit up. All that thick black smoke turned to dark red with flashes of yellow, white, blue streaks of flames that danced on the ceiling like a Broadway show. We turned to get out, and the nozzle man's turnout coat got hooked up to a drop ceiling cable. I helped him get it unhooked, and we made it out. The chief told us to take the line to the second floor and hit the pockets of fire that were pushing up from the store below. You see most of the fire was in the ceiling on the first floor, weakening the second floor as we stood on it. The brothers from Rescue 3 came up with saws and were opening holes in the floor looking for fire. When they found a spot we could hit with the hose, the two brothers started cutting but you couldn't see anything because of the smoke and the fact that the electric was off. This went on for five minutes when all of a sudden the chief comes running up the stairs screaming *"Mayday!"*(Firefighter in danger or missing). Then all the radios were going *Mayday!! Mayday!! A firefighter went through the roof!* We were on the top floor. We put down the line and started to search every inch of that shop looking for the brother or a hole in the ceiling. There were brothers all over the place. Finally, we hear the radio call that they have found the brother in the store below us. He had walked around the counter on the 2nd floor and fell head first 15 feet to the floor below. A piece of concrete hit him in the back of the head and killed him instantly. His body was found face down in a foot of water. The brothers were performing CPR on him all the way to the hospital where he was pronounced dead. It was surreal walking out to the street after the fire was knocked down and see the emotion on the brother's faces.

I went over to one of the brothers and asked him how he looked, and he just held his head down and said "not good." We hugged and said a prayer for the brother and his family. The officer saw my finger was pointing in two different directions and told me to get the finger checked, so I tapped out with a broken finger, hating every minute of it because we just lost one of New York's bravest. It was a night of praying and talking about a job that was the perfect storm. You see the landlord had done illegal renovations behind the counter where the brother stepped. The floor got weakened by the fire in the ceiling below. I went to the funeral, and it was a tough day! Seeing his children and wife and family crying was just too much. It was also a wake-up call to me that this was one of the most dangerous jobs in the world, and as firefighters we were not indestructible. I would realize this in the years to come that you could die at any moment on this job and we the FDNY are the best and the busiest fire department in the world and we just had one of our brothers die in a fire. After the fire, the counseling unit came around to the firehouses and was talking to the brothers, but I never got any counseling I was in the hospital getting my finger set. I now know that the best counseling was right in the firehouse...the brothers!

A couple of weeks went by, and Dave came over to visit with my cousin. Everything was so fresh in my head. I dreamed about that night for months after. Dave comes over to me and starts, *"So Chris, how is the fire department treating you... getting much sleep?"* My insides were like a box of firecrackers being lit by a match. I went off on him hard! *"Yea Dave..., Sleep!!... I just lost a good friend at a fire in the Bronx while you were in bed sleeping! Tell me, Dave, when was the last time you had to carry one of your professors out of the classroom and watch him die in front of you!!-- then go to the funeral and watch his young kids holding their fathers helmet and his wife holding the flag that was just covering the casket carrying her husband's body and crying every step of the way!! – knowing that the children will be without a father and she will never share time with the man she loves!!"* Dave just took a step back and said, *"Chris, I am so sorry for your loss. I didn't know."* I told him every day we go to work we put our lives on the line for total strangers, some are good people, some are bad people, people who hate us. We put our lives on the line for them knowing we may never make it home! After our talk, Dave turned out to be a caring person. I would find out just how much he changed for the better a couple years later on September 11, 2001...

6

Where the Action Is—Engine 42

I worked in Ladder 46 truck for three years. When I first got there, an officer in the engine called me into his office and told me that whatever I did, do not listen to anyone in the truck. He was an old time Irish lieutenant who hated the truckies for one reason or another. He told me they don't know shit about fire duty and that if I had any questions to come to him. Now, I am a bit of a young guy and had never really been exposed to this type of back stabbing. This was a first in my life, and the first time at a workplace. You see when I started to work at my first job at 18, I worked as a house painter, and I didn't know anything about painting houses, but I had to act as I knew and at the end of the day my boss asked me if I knew anything about painting. I told him "no" but I need a job. From there I worked every job known to man. I worked as a fireplace installer, worked in a factory called Avon making beauty products, as a beer salesman (thank God I didn't drink). I worked as a bridge painter, and that was a trip! Then I left the bridge and went to work for my brother as an exterminator in Manhattan (that's a whole other book...lol). I also worked side jobs and even worked as a male dancer and other odd jobs to make ends meet. I had taken every civil servant test out there, Post Office, State Police, NYPD test, and, of course, the FDNY twice. I had to take the test twice. In 1977, I passed the written and the physical part and then women protested the test, so they made changes to the physical test to allow more women to get the job, leaving me waiting for seven more years till I took the test in '84 and passed. The rest is history. I had twice been subjected to reverse discrimination. First was the State Police test when I received a phone call at work one day, and the voice on the phone told me that I could not fight the Supreme Court, and as a young kid I believed him and never got called. Then again with the fire department. I had been knocked down quite a few times in my life looking for jobs. I think all the while it was setting me up to be a firefighter. You see I could have walked away from all the disappointments in my life and just quit, but the fire department doesn't hire quitters. To work as a firefighter, you have to have a *"don't take no for an answer", a "never give up" attitude.* You are faced with things that normal people would not even think of doing, but you jump in head-first. It's that stretching a charged hose down a smoked filled room or building. It's taking a beating because you cannot see as it's getting real hot in the room. It's doing a search in a room where you have to feel the walls so you can find your way out, all while taking a physical beating from the smoke, fire, and the heat. It's that push of "don't quit" that makes a great firefighter-almost like a superhero except we cannot fly. I worked in the truck for three years, but my love for the job was on the inside battling the red devil. I transferred to an Engine; it was the fourth busiest in the city. It was Engine 42, also known as the "O.K. Corral" because of a shooting that happened a few years before I got there. They

33

had a livery cab driver take out his anger on the brothers. He walked up to the firehouse while the brothers were standing out front and started shooting! Everywhere the brothers ran this guy shot. If it weren't for the fact that his gun jammed, it could have been a lot worse. Engine 42 was the place for me and a place where God put me and wanted me to be. The fire duty was incredible. There were nights when we would get two or three jobs (fires) in a 24-hour shift. The neighborhood was tough with a narrow one-way street with shootings and stabbings, crime and drug dealing and just plain evil! But through all of the bad, there were little kids growing up in this mess of evil, kids with no fathers, parents who were drug addicts or alcoholics. There were arguments and screaming in the streets, plus drug trafficking all hours of the night. This was the action I had been looking for... to be in a company with a great reputation as an aggressive firefighting company!!

7

You Can Never Let Your Guard Down

What I learned in the three years in the truck is nothing compared to the experiences of the next five years in Engine 42. The first thing you have to do in a new house is to earn the respect of the brothers. You see coming over from a truck to an engine is usually unheard of, but between God and the way things worked out I knew I was in the right place. The first thing I knew about 42 was that it was the busiest house, and they did a great job that earned the respect of other firehouses and firefighters throughout the FDNY. They were a single engine company working in a big area. When we got a job, you knew there wouldn't be a truck responding for a few minutes, leaving us to stretch the line and maybe force the apartment door and do a quick search till the truck showed up. One of my first jobs was to stretch a line to an exposer (side of a building on fire). When I got off the rig (engine), one of the brothers started to scream at me to get a 1"3/4 hose...Right then and there I knew this was going to take some getting used to. After the fire was knocked down, I spoke to the brother privately and told him don't ever talk to me like that again. He said that you have to learn how we work in 42; we have our own way of doing things. I told him, so do I and it's not to scream at someone in the street during a job-- it doesn't help! Guys came over to me and said you were right to tell him that because he likes to get inside new guys heads. I told the brothers I don't know if he wants to go there because I scare myself. Now I know from being on the job for three years that you are going to work with some great guys, and you are going to work with guys you just don't care for. 99.9% of the guys you work with are the greatest; it's that 1% that you are not going to care for one reason or another. Within the first few weeks and months, we were running in and out between fires, car accidents (we were right off the Cross Bronx Expressway) shootings, stabbings and other emergencies. The action was great but sometimes crazy.

Within the first couple of months I was at 42, the biggest thing I realized is that it's a one-way street, and you are a couple of stores from the corner where drugs are pushed every minute. Then you see the kids who have to live with all this crime. You could pick out the bad and the good in a minute and see that good people would get up and head to work anywhere between 5 am to 8 am every morning. Then like clockwork you would see the same people come home between 4 pm and 7 pm. This was every day and sometimes on weekends. I would say hello to everyone and greet them in the morning. I tried to make friends with everyone I met. I made some great friends on that block.

Some of the greatest people I have ever met in my life- Mr. and Mrs. Gibson a man in his late 80's from Georgia. I would meet them outside the firehouse as Mr. Gibson and his friend Leroy Abersom would get the morning paper from the bodega. They would tell me stories of how it used to be on the block before all the drugs came in. They would tell me how they would sleep in the park overnight, and no one would bother them. *"Those were the days,"* they used to say all the time. They were right!! These two men were great friends. Mr. Gibson would take care of his grandchildren because his son had problems. I would see Mrs. Gibson walking them to church every Sunday dressed to the tee. Mr. Gibson passed away a few years later, and Mrs. Gibson followed a month later. I went to both their funerals in Harlem. I told Leroy she died from a broken heart. I miss them very much! They don't make them like that anymore.

There was another woman who I became friends with, Gloria and Jim an old Italian couple. Gloria was a funny woman always singing and drawing on the sidewalk leaving messages for the brothers, like *"Good morning gentlemen, God watch over you."* She would bake cookies. I became good friends with her. Then, Jimmy, her husband, passed away, and she became lost in a tough neighborhood, but we always stayed close to her and protected her from some of the bad in the neighborhood. After her husband had died, she got mad at one of the brothers and spray-painted his old van silver from the wheels to the roof. When we had a run later that night, he saw his van and had to laugh. He said she must be out of paint because as we looked down the block she had painted the telephone poles, and the manhole covers silver!! We called the brother's van the Silver Streak!! Years later, Leroy called me and told me she was in the hospital; they think she had a heart attack. I was home but ran down to the hospital in the Bronx and seen her laying in the hallway. I went over to her, and she gave me a hug and said she had been in the hallway for five hours, so I went over to the nurse and asked when will my grandmother get a room? Since I was a firefighter, she got a room in about 15 minutes. We went up to the room together and laughed about all the old times from the neighborhood and I asked her if she has anymore spray-paint. She just laughed. I gave

her a kiss and a hug and told her to call me if
she needed anything. She passed away a week
later. I love the time we had together; she was
funniest women I think I have ever met. Love
you, Gloria!!

 I think it was more of letting them know that I
cared about them. The kids were the most
important to me because they had no one to
look up to. I started to realize that being a
firefighter gave you the chance to make a
positive influence in someone's life. These kids
didn't stand a chance without showing them
that there was someone who cared about them.
The drugs in the neighborhood were handed
down by generations of families that ran the
block. There was flashy money all around. The
dealers had nice cars, jewelry, cash, nice
clothes, and expensive sneakers. The
temptation was always right in front of their
faces. I would tell some of the kids that these
people are not good people. They would argue
that these dealers protect the neighborhood. I
would explain to them the dealers bring bad
people in and cause pain to others and their

families. They were around this type of living, and they just didn't understand. Then one day I was waiting for one of the brothers to come to work. He was running late because he was coaching his daughter's softball team. I was standing outside. It was in June of 1990, and it was a hot summer evening with music playing and people in the street hanging at the corner and others coming home from work, others sitting playing domino's while others were playing cards. There were two kids about ten and eight years old playing baseball with a rolled up piece of paper wrapped in tape, so I went to the trunk of my car and got out a Spaulding ball that I would play with my kids. I started pitching to the kids, and they were hitting it back to me when all of a sudden I heard loud pops going off up near the corner. I thought to myself that it must be fireworks figuring that the locals were celebrating the 4th of July early. I continued to play ball with the kids, but then I looked across the one-way street and seen the bricks turning into dust at the same time. I thought there were fireworks going off, then I noticed people lying on the sidewalk covering their heads and others running down the block from the corner. As I turned to see what was going on, I couldn't believe my eyes!! There was a young Spanish kid with a submachine gun sweeping both sides of the street leaving me and these two kids out in the open. I grabbed the two kids and rolled behind a double parked car. The kids asked me what the matter was, and I told them there is a guy with a gun shooting the streets up. They were scared, but I told them I was going to make a run for the firehouse door that was about 25 feet away from where we were. I looked up at the kid with the gun, and he was changing the clip. I took off from behind the car, and the shooter pushed the clip in and began shooting. As I ran for the door with both kids under my arms, in my head I was dodging bullets. I punched in the combo and opened the door pushing the two kids, telling them that we were safe now. I went in the back where all the brothers were sitting at the kitchen table and told them about the major shooting out front. They said they heard the shots. I told them I was trapped behind a car while the kid was shooting and that he hit a lot of people. I told them that we have to get out there. One of the brothers turned to me stating that we are not cops, and we have no guns. I looked out the window near the door, and there were people all over the street. I said the shooting stopped. We all ran out grabbing rubber gloves and all our first aid bags and started working on the victims. There were people shot on both sides of the street. The most severe was a man in the middle of the street. Blood was pumping out of a bullet hole in his chest. One of the brothers pushed his fingers into the hole to stop the bleeding, but the man had lost too much blood and died at the scene. Another victim shot and fell into a Chinese restaurant and covered the floor with blood. His friends threw him into a car and took him to the hospital. There was a victim who went in for cover in a liquor store and bled out when we went in to help him. There was about an inch of blood covering the floor in the doorway. There was a total of six victims! We later found out that this kid, the shooter, killed two people who were innocent victims while walking home from work. I prayed for those people. The other people shot were all working with the big drug dealer on the block. They were the old men that were bums or alcoholics and would watch out for police. They would sit near the bodega next to an empty box, underneath would be where the drugs were, and the runners would go and pick up the crack, heroin, weed or whatever the drug was that the dealers would sell it to the people. I didn't feel sorry for them. You see when you dance with the devil, he always leads to no good! The Police Department showed up, and I was a witness to the shooting. They took my statement, and only one woman came forward and gave a statement as well, no one wanted to get involved. My description was a young Latin male between the ages of 15 to 17 years of age with a slight build, weight about 145 to 150, stood about 5'9" had a slight mustache and black hair. The block was closed off for hours as the NYPD did the investigation and the company was put out of service till they finished up. The brother came in that I was holding up for, and he was so glad I was alright. The captain was a covering officer. He called me into the office and told me he was going to put me in for a medal. He wrote up the paper that I still have. You see in 42, they never believed in individual medals it was always the company. The family of the two boys came over to thank me and were so glad that the boys were safe. Later that family moved off the block to the suburbs in New Jersey getting away. A week or so went by and the cops stopped in with some photos of a couple of suspects, but they were not the shooter. Then one day a car pulls up across the street from the firehouse and a kid gets out of the car as the driver remained in the car. They were parked in a way that blocked the Engine from getting out, so as the guy gets out of the car he gives us the stare down. One of the brothers asked what his problem was, and the guy smiled and kept walking. Another brother tells the driver to move the car, so he moves the car down a couple of feet. Now I see the guy getting back into the car, and I say, " *Damn that guy looks familiar.*" I write down the plate number as the kid gets in the car. He takes his fingers and makes it out to be a gun and pretends to shoot us all. That's when we called the police, and they ran the plate. A couple of days later they caught the guy by the license plate I gave them. The guy came back in the neighborhood to intimidate me by saying I can come and kill you anytime I want. The word in the street was that the kid, 16 years old was trying to kill the head drug dealer and take over his corner or territory. The testimony he gave the police was that the dealer disrespected his sister, and he wanted to get back at the dealer. Within the next month or so the dealer got a new license plate, and it read *"Hard2Kill."* His car was a 69 Thunderbird mint condition with white leather seats and a cherry red color. Now you see what I was up against and why I never stopped trying to help those kids in that neighborhood!

8

Paula and *"The Package is in the Mail"*

At this point I wished I had more time in my schedule and my personal life. We worked a tour that was two days of 9 am to 6 pm. After, you would come in for two-night tours from 6 pm to 9 am, but we could work a 24-hour tour that would give you a day and a half off. Being in the neighborhood every day was impossible but some of the brothers would talk to the kids when they could. Some of the brothers who were there for a year didn't even know the people in the neighborhood's names. I started shoveling the snow off of the sidewalks for the older people. Then some of the brothers would shovel the walkways when I wasn't in. So maybe some of the good rubbed off on some of them. The neighborhood was a mix of races, religions and nationalities. The further you got away from the corner the better the people, or so I thought. There was a family that lived right next to the firehouse. The only thing that separated the two buildings was an alleyway about 5 feet wide. In the house lived a middle age Jewish guy and his Puerto Rican wife, Larry and Sonia. He was a big time hunter, and she was a housewife who was always well dressed. In the downstairs apartment there was a couple with four kids. They were all related. Now down the block lived Sonia's son and daughter-in-law. It was her son from another marriage and he worked for the city. One day the women introduced me to her daughter-in-law's sister Paula who came over from Puerto Rico. She was never in the country, and I think the family was trying to get her a husband. I showed her around the city and introduced her to some brothers, and we became friends. One day I was getting off work, and she called me over because she smelled smoke in the house and wasn't sure where it was coming from. We went upstairs, and I looked around and found a fluorescent light was flickering, and I told her it was the smell of the ballast in the light, so I took the light out, and the phone rang while I was standing there. I heard her say, *"the package was mailed out."* Now this guy was an avid big game hunter. He went over to Africa to hunt big game and had animals in his house a 7' grizzly bear, a cape buffalo head mounted on the wall, a stuffed leopard; you get the idea. She tells me that Larry and Sonia (not their real names) went to the Dominican Republic for a month and that Larry told her that if anyone calls that she was to say, *"The package was mailed."* I thought this was strange, but what did I know? They were good working people well-respected in the neighborhood. I would never have suspected anything wrong, but then as I was leaving Paula (not her real name) said to me, *"Chris, do you want to see Larry's gun room?"* I was curious, so I said ok, but when I looked around the room I felt as though something was not right. I didn't want to see it but she insisted and opened up one of the boxes and showed me the gun, but I told her I really didn't want to see it. The room was locked up with a padlock. She opened the room it was 10 feet by 10 feet and full of stacked boxes in piles almost to the ceiling. Paula said they were the boxes that she was to say *"were in the mail"* to the callers. There were hundreds of boxes and in the boxes were guns. After seeing the room, I had a feeling that something was not right. Well during the next couple of days we had the fire where the brother from Rescue 3 was killed... the story I told you about where I was on medical leave with the broken finger. Well, I get a call from one of the brothers during the week that I was on medical leave, and they asked me, *"Did you get arrested?"* Now I know by now not to take the bait and laughed. They said no, you didn't hear what happen to Larry and Sonia? *I said no! What's going on?* They said the FBI and the Alcohol & Tobacco (ATF) asked if they could use the roof of the firehouse to do surveillance of the building next to the firehouse. Larry and Sonia's house, because they were selling guns to drug dealers. The brothers said they raided the house and arrested Paula and the family on the first floor and put them all in handcuffs and took them away. Now the room made sense to me! The hundreds of boxes of guns in the room all locked up and Paula answering the phone and Larry telling her to say, *"The package is in the mail."* The FBI/ATF arrested her son, and

Larry and Sonia were arrested in Puerto Rico. Later I received a letter from Paula that she was released from jail, and she told me what happened. Larry was selling guns to dealers throughout the Islands, and the package he sent went to the wrong address in Puerto Rico and a woman opened it and brought it to the post office and tracked it back to Larry's address. Turns out the person on the phone while I was in the house was an undercover agent checking the return number. This is how Paula got arrested but let go. Larry told the feds that Paula had nothing to do with it, but she could no longer come back into the United States. Well when I got back to work after the finger healed, the brothers were primed up with some great material!! They had pictures of me in a prison suit. They went out and got a "Most Wanted" poster from the post office and put my picture on it. They greeted me when I came into the kitchen wearing their shirts over their head covering their faces doing the "perp walk" (with members of the media usually in attendance...short for "perpetrator walk,") You see besides being great at fighting fires and at their side jobs, they are amazing at editing photos. I gave them so much material that it lasted a long time. This was a case where I could have been at the wrong place at the wrong time. Larry and Sonia had their house seized by the government and sold at auction. I always had a thought in my head about where that kid who shot six people in the neighborhood killing two innocent victims got his gun from! Larry?

9

Love, Abuse and the Neighborhood

You see as time went on as I worked in 42, some of the local people would try and get over on me. Some people took kindness as weakness, but with me it was all from the heart. I truly cared for some of them, not so much for the bad people on the block, but the old saying keep your friends close and your enemies closer. The kids were number one on my list of people that I cared and worried about. These kids didn't choose to live like this nor did they have a chance to pick their parents. So they dealt with the life on the block, really not knowing any better. When I was at work, I would always talk to them and guide them. I could see that if I was going to make a difference. I was going to have to work real hard with them. Anytime they wanted to talk I would listen; anytime they needed advice I gave it. I would have mothers come over to the firehouse in the morning and ask me to walk their kids to school because they didn't want to go. I would tell the brothers I am walking down the block to the school and if we get a run, just pick me up at the end of the block. Any time I was asked to walk the kids down the block we never got a run. I think God knew that I was trying to do His work. There were homeless people walking through the hood, and you had no idea where they came from. This was part of the runners (drugs) change over. Then you would have the locals that were there all the time never working or doing the bare minimum to survive. There was a woman with three daughters ranging in the ages of 16,18,19 and each one of them had two children except for the 16-year-old, she had one child, but the older two had two children each from different guys. All the mothers were doing was collecting SSI for all of them. They were another check in the mail. Crazy! There was a real hard working Mexican family that all their children lived at home and commuted to work every day. They were a great family. They later bought two more buildings on the block and gave it to their children. The Mexican's daughter asked me if I would marry her to become a citizen. Not that I was some good looking guy, I think it was more of a bi-weekly paycheck with benefits. The family offered me $5000. I turned it down. You see my personal life was a mess. I had just gotten custody of my daughter and son in the late 80's from a relationship where I was married at 18. The marriage was destined to fail, two young kids in a rough world trying to survive and raise a family, the odds were against us. It was a crazy, stressful time in my life. I was a kid when I got married right out of high school. I went from a young man looking at colleges and sending high school football films to coaches, to a young man trying to be a father overnight. The marriage was over after ten years and two children. Then after a couple of years of separation, I got custody of my son and daughter. I was a young man trying to figure life out, and now I would be raising my children on my own. Thank God for my parents because I couldn't have done it without them. To my mother and father, I owe everything because they became more of my children's parents. I was running back and forth from the firehouse to home all along trying to find a place in the New York City Fire Department. A job that you needed to have your head and soul in at all times. Then at the same time trying to find a place and an identity in the firehouse and life. All along the way, wanting to have a family, feeling like a failure that the relationship ended. So instead of working on me as a father, I was worried about my feelings as a person. That was the wrong path to take.

During the years I was in the 89, I met a girl who lived a couple of blocks from the firehouse. She seemed like a person who I could start a family with, but now my life was going to get real crazy. You see all along the way I was getting messages that I did not pay attention to. I was blinded by the thought of raising a family with someone who I thought I got along with; instead she was someone who had no interest in raising a family. She became pregnant with my third child. All along I thought it would all come together, and I would have that family. I was mistaken! It was to become the most stressful time of my life. My third child was born in 1990, my first year E42. My son was born in August. The relationship with his mother was very physically abusive. I had been slapped, punched, things thrown at me, verbally abused. I took it and never laid a hand on her throughout the relationship. I was in such a blinded search for a family and afraid of another failed relationship that I overlooked all the abuse and started blaming myself for her behavior. I didn't know any better and like the kids on the block, they didn't know better either. You see abuse is a strange thing. After a while, you start to blame yourself for the actions of the other person striking out at you. Like the abuse the kids took on the street to the abuse behind closed doors and some that carried out into the streets, you could tell by their actions which kids were the ones who were being abused. Some of them walked with the scars on their faces and others in their hearts.

There was a couple of little brothers about age 11 or 12 years old that had a pit bull. They would tie the dog to a chain link fence and beat the dog with rolled up newspapers. The dog would be barking and showing his teeth and snapping at the two of them. Every time they would hit the dog, I went out there and told them to leave the dog alone. I asked them how would they like it if someone did that to them? They just gave me the look. I realized what they were doing. They were taking their anger and pain out on the dog. These were two kids that I would later walk to school and give advice to. You could see how angry some of the kids were, by the way, they treated their dogs. Like in life, the children couldn't pick their parents no more than the dog could pick his owner. There was a little kid that owned a white German shepherd the likes of which I have never seen since. He would walk the dog with a bathrobe tie. When we walked up the block, you could see the poor dog was scared because this little kid would beat the dog. One day this little boy and another kid got into a fight. I heard the screaming in front of the firehouse and went outside to see these two boys squaring off. One of the brothers came to the front of the firehouse to help me break it up. The moment I opened the door this white German shepherd ran in the firehouse hiding behind turnout coats up against the wall shivering from fright. We went out and broke the fight up telling each kid to walk the other way. Just then the kid with the white shepherd said, "Chris where is my dog?" I told him he must have run down the street. He said no. He went into the firehouse. I told him to look around, and he did, but the dog was so afraid of going back with this kid that he couldn't be found. So the kid leaves and I go in the back to tell the brothers that there was a dog in the firehouse that was afraid to leave. One of the brothers told me to leave him here; someone will take him and give him a good home. I went to get ready to go home when one of the brothers came over to me and started asking why this dog was in the house. I told him what one of the senior men told me... that someone would take the dog home. The dog was being beaten by the kid in the street. He started raising his voice to me and said to get him out. I looked in disbelief. *I said the dog was getting abused!*! He told me he didn't care and to let him out. I said you want to throw that dog out of the firehouse, it will never make it. So I left. I drove down the street and around the corner and back up to see if he let the dog out and sure enough there was the kid with the white shepherd on the bath tie walking with his dog. I was pissed!! I came back in for my next tour, and one of the brothers told me what had happened a couple of days earlier. The NYPD swat team came to the building down the block with animal control agents and two vans full of swat members in full armor. They went to the roof of the building, and there were two pit bulls on the roof top and the super called the cops about not being able to get out on the roof. The cops stopped down at the firehouse to tell the brothers what was going on. They said that there were two fighting pit bulls on the roof and that they had to take down because someone threw a white German Shepherd out at them and the two pit bulls tore the dog apart!! I was so mad at the asshole (brother... I use that term loosely) who let him out. The next time he came in I wanted to kick his ass!! I called him out and told him to go down the basement. The basement is where if you have a problem with someone you take it to the basement and fight it out. It's an unwritten rule that's been in the firehouse for centuries, but he refused- saying that he would not go downstairs with me and that I should leave the animals outside the firehouse. He sat down on the chair and wouldn't get up to face the challenge. Remember 99.9% of the brothers are great people. One percent are not so nice. Well here was one of the one percent. It was tough to work with someone like that. You see what happened to that poor dog was no one took the time to help or save him from the streets, the abuse, and the violence on the block. Guys like that turn their back not only on the people but also on the kids of the block. That's why some of us tried to make a difference in a kid's life. I started to see the kids on the block like that, the beautiful white German shepherd, innocent, afraid, helpless, abused, looking for help and the streets tearing them apart like those pit bulls did with people turning their backs on them. I promised myself that I would never turn my back on these kids on the block.

10

Learning the Ropes- Earning the Brother's Respect!

If you had four rooms on fire, you would start at the door and work your way in; taking one room at a time staying as low as you could because the temperature a foot above your head could kill you or put you in the burn center for months. The jobs were picking up. It was a busy time we were running about 5300 runs a year. All four seasons were always busy. The winter was the toughest because everyone had their windows closed and you couldn't see the fire till it blew out windows. During the summer, everyone had windows open, and you could see the smoke as you were getting near the building. We were mixing between EMS runs and fires duties. It was crazy at times, but I would not change a thing. If we were not fighting fires, then we were responding to shooting victims and other emergencies. Every day was a different story. You see I could not have worked at a desk job or a factory... just not enough action. Here you could go from giving CPR to someone and saving their life, to balls to the wall fire and battling the *Red Devil "Monster"* who doesn't care who stands in his way. You see fire would dance around you while you fought it. When you had more than four rooms of fire, you had to go room to room and stay low. If you went to stand up, you would be burnt from the heat alone in a matter of feet. The temperature can range from 1100 degrees on the ceiling and the closer you get to the floor the cooler it gets, but that could be 500 to 300 hundred degrees, so you have to be on your knees the whole time advancing the line till you knock down the fire. In the Engine everyone has positions that they are assigned to. Only the chauffeur would hook up to the hydrant (johnny pump for the old timers). The control man would assist the chauffeur on the hookup and then work his way inside (this position will be taken away a few years later from the Engines).

Then you have the doorman he stays in the doorway and feeds the line in on the advance, and then the backup man who helps take the physical pressure of the hose and help out with moving the line (hose) forward so that the nozzle man has someone to lean on. Then there is the greatest position!!-- The spot that all the brothers in the Engine want (And some of the truck guys, they just wouldn't admit it) the *Nozzleman, the Knob*!! This was the action spot!! There is an unwritten rule that you never give up the Knob. You see in the Engine I worked in, it was not assigned spots when you had the seat next to the door on the engine (rig) which was called the jump seat. It was first one to the back step gets the Nozzle, which added to the aggressiveness of the company. Nothing like all the guys hustling to the back step. As a Nozzleman and backup you could take a beating between the cold water hitting the heat and fire, then coming back down on you like hot tea water. Guys would get burns on their face, nose, ears, knees; anywhere there was no protection. There were a few times where I got burns on my knees, wrist and ears. They were like second degree burns, usually a blister. One of the brothers spent a couple of weeks in the burn center with bad burns on the face and neck. He had the Knob and went to the end of a hallway in an apartment and could not advance the line. He saw the fire at the top of the ceiling and moved the lineup closer to the wall hitting the ceiling when all of a sudden that water came down like hot tea water hitting him on the face and ears. When he got outside, his skin was peeling off his ears and part of his neck. These are the actions you could never get at a desk in an office. He was burnt really bad because of the crazy renovation in the apartment. The Super (maintenance man) put a wall up in a hallway to make another room. So besides going into a fire in a smoked filled room, you are also battling illegal renovations. You just never knew. There are areas that you are assigned to where firehouses are *first due* to the area. If there is a fire and the *first due* company gets delayed, *you don't wait*!

We were out doing inspections on buildings when a run (fire) came in. It was in the middle of the day on Jerome Avenue in the Bronx. It was a five bay auto repair garage up in flames. We were right there, so we beat the *first due* company. I jumped off the rig and got the Knob and started stretching it to the bays. The fire was so intense that the metal gates were melting and dropping balls of fire to the ground. I got the 2 1/2-inch hose used to push out a lot of water on fires like this. The only problem was the chauffeur had us running off booster water from the 500-gallon tank on the engine since we did not have a hydrant yet. The problem with this is you use the water faster. He was getting ready to hook up the hydrant. I had already made my move in the garage hitting the ceiling and the ground to move the fireballs falling from the gate. My backup man was a brother who I went to high school with. We were pushing the line in when we get about halfway in and the water shuts down- major trouble!! They were hooking up to the engine, and we were without water for about 30 seconds which felt like an hour in the garage with the red devil dancing all around us. It was like it was spitting fireballs at us from above. Finally, we got water and made our advance, not being able to see anything but fire. I was doing what we call a duck walk where you stay close to the floor and squat as you walked like...yes... like a duck! I went to kneel to adjust, and my knee hit a fireball of melted metal gate. Damn!! I said to the brother, "I just got burnt." He said, "Give me the line!!" I said, "Hell no!!" and moved in further, then got up to where four cars were on fire in the garage knocking the fire down. Then I went to kneel on the other knee.... ssssssssssttt. *Damn...* I told the brother I just got burnt on the other knee. He said, "Give me the knob!!" I said, "No way!! "We ended up in a spot where we were leaning on an object while hitting pockets of fire when the roofman vented the roof and smoke started to clear. The brother wanted to get the hell back when he seen we were leaning on a hydraulic lift with a car on it. You see this is the danger you face. Every time you fight the *Red Devil*, he/she is always looking for a victim to consume or destroy. When I got out, I had been burnt twice on both knees. They were 2nd-degree burns. It was a *"Welcome to the big show Kid!!"* The brothers came over asking who had the Knob. One of the brothers said Chris, "Wow nice job kid!! Now right then and there, I realized that was the way to earn the brothers respect!

11

A Day in the Life

When you are subjected to all this death and mayhem on the streets, you start to realize that life is short. At any time, you could be caught in a crossfire or could be seriously hurt or even killed in a fire. So when you are in the safe confines of the firehouse you want to laugh and keep things light. When you're not drilling on how to handle fires at least twice a day; you are keeping the firehouse clean. In the morning, we would have to make beds, clean all the bathrooms, the kitchen, the officer's room, mopping and cleaning toilets was all part of the job. It's called committee work everyone had to help out. Some guys would check the rigs (engine or truck) making sure that all the equipment was in good condition and in working order. The Scott packs (air packs that give us air to go into smoky fires). This has to be checked every tour. Usually, the junior man would do it, but you should never trust anybody with the only thing that's going to keep you alive in a fire. When committee work was over, you would sit down to study. We would train on all sorts of ways to fight fires in the buildings in our area where we worked, like a multiple dwelling, private houses, high rises, h-type buildings, taxpayers (stories) even operating at a car fire and accidents on the highways. There was just so much to learn. Working near a highway was always dangerous!

One night on the Cross Bronx Expressway about 3:30 am, we got a call for a four car accident on the westbound side. When we pulled up an engine and a truck company was all set up on the westbound side. The chauffeur pulled up on the eastbound side to protect an EMS ambulance who had pulled over on the shoulder to pick up injured passengers from the cars and the roadway. People were ejected from cars. There were about six victims, two critical conditions. The captain from the first due engine called for another ambulance (Bus is the term we use) to respond to this accident. EMS pulled up and parked behind the engine. There were cones set up behind the rig (engine). We were bringing the last of the victims over the center concrete divider. There were four of us (brothers) and a woman EMT. As we lifted the injured victim and put him in the ambulance as the EMT is shutting the doors and the four of us were climbing over the divide, we hear a loud bang that sounded like a bomb then a scream of someone who was in a severe pain!! We turn around, and a car drove right through the cones and crashed into the back of the ambulance pinning the EMT up against the concrete divider crushing her hips, pelvis, and legs. We jumped over the guard rail as a cop went to the driver of the car, it was two women, the passenger was sleeping, and the driver was holding the wheel thinking she was still moving not even knowing she had just crashed her car into the back of the ambulance almost killing five first responders. We were seconds away from all of us being killed or seriously injured! The cop started screaming at the driver. He reached in and took the key out and put the car in park. The driver was so drunk. She was still holding the wheel. He asked her what her problem was, and she said, "nothing I am driving home mom." She thought she was hearing her mother's voice. This lasted for a second because the officer dragged her out the window of the driver's side. We all jumped over the guard rail, and two brothers held the EMT up as we all picked up the car off of her. I will never forget her death screams of pain. We had to get another ambulance for her and for the victim in that bus already. Thank God he was strapped into the stretcher. We finished up and started heading back to quarters joking about how close we all came to losing our legs or even our lives. You see that's what we had to do, keep things "real" in emergencies, but light in real life! I said a prayer for the EMT but never thanked God for saving my life or the lives of the brothers.... God saw I didn't get it yet!! When we got back to quarters it was the start of the day shift; we were operating at that accident for over four hours. It was another day in the O.K. Corral....

When you came in on a day shift, it was a rule that you brought something in for breakfast for the brothers on the night tour. Everyone, well almost everyone, the square rooters (Someone always trying to get over), or the Hairbags (someone who complains about everything), would stop at a bakery or a bagel place or pick up eggs and bacon. It was an unwritten rule!! If someone didn't, his balls were busted all day!! The responsibility of the meals and the house watch (answer phones and greeting people knocking at the door and turning out companies responding to fires and other emergencies). This was done 24 hours a day. You get no breaks in a busy firehouse. In double houses, these were split between the Truck and the Engine. In single companies, it came down to everyone would have to step up (help out). You see the majority picked the meals. If you are in on the meals, you are in for every meal for your career. We would have to share the expense for the food. Five guys would divide the cost. Whether you ate it hot or cold-- nothing worse than a cold cheeseburger... meaning if you get a run you are out of luck. You still had to pay. Same with dinner, tough eating a steak that was sitting for an hour!! That's where you learned to eat quickly. Sometimes you would get a square rooter or a Seagull (the brother who's out on the meal but eats the leftovers) who would never be in on the meals and not pay to cause all the brothers to pay more per man. But in the middle of the night he would come down and eat the leftovers. We knew this!! So one night we had meatballs one of the brothers took atom hot sauce and cut a hole in it and pumped the hot stuff in it LOL!! The next morning this officer was in the bathroom all night!! He ate a meatball sandwich. He had heartburn all day long sitting on the toilet and pounding down tums!! We laughed all day long. You see you watch out for one another it's an unwritten rule!!

12

Death, Birth and Saving Lives

 What some people don't see in a lifetime, I would see in two 24 hour tours. It all started on the night tour (6-9). We get an EMS run for a person shot around the block from the firehouse. As we responded, people were standing around a body lying on the sidewalk face down in a puddle of blood around the victim's head. I got off the rig with the EMS bag. You see we got trained for the first responder because we were faster than the bus (ambulance) so we were expected to give the victims a chance to make it (live). As I got up to the body, I could see he was a young man about 17 years of age. I could see that he's shot in the back of the head. The blood was puddling around his head. He was laying on his stomach, and the left side of his face was on the sidewalk.

As I bent down down to check his pulse, one of
the brothers said to leave him. He is dead. As
he said that, a bubble of blood was coming out
of this kid's nose. It started as a small bubble
and got bigger and bigger. I told the brother he
was breathing. I said there was an air bubble
coming out of his nose. The officer came over to
look, and we watched as the bubble popped!!
That was it. That young man just died right in
front of us, and we saw his last breath. I got
back on the rig, and one of the brothers said,
*"You cannot save the world. These people are
killing one another, and there is nothing you can
do about it."* EMS got there and waited for a
paramedic to make contact with a doctor to
pronounce him dead!! A waste of a life shot in
the back of the head, 17 years old … gone!!
When we left the scene, it was back to normal.
One of the brothers said, "Hey let's get
dinner!!" … "What do you guys feel like eating?"
I thought to myself, I just saw this young guy
take his last breath, and we are worried about
dinner! So I finished my prayer for his soul and
then I said, "Who wants chicken parm?" They
all said, "I am in!!" You see we all acted like it
was just another day at the office. That picture

stuck in my mind for a long time; that bubble of blood, full of that guy's last breath burst!!

The next day on the day tour (9-6), we get another EMS run. We drove around the block where the shooting victim died the night before and head to a Brownstone (a type of brick they made houses out of 3 stories) There is a black woman sitting on the stairs. We get off the rig and ask her if she called the Fire Dept.? She said I didn't say fire! I told them my sister is having a baby! She told us to follow her. We got up to the 2nd floor in the back bedroom where there was a big woman lying on her back with her legs bent like she was giving birth. She said I need an ambulance, not firemen. I told her we were the best that she was going to get right now. We all looked at one another, and I put on the gloves and told her to remove the blanket from her legs. When she did, I could see the baby's head crowning. I asked her if she has any other children and she said yes six children. I felt a big relief that she had been through this a few times and knew what to do. So I asked her to push, as she did, the baby's head came out to the neck. I placed my hand on the side of the

77

head and told her to push again. Now the shoulders came out. I told her one more push and out came this beautiful baby girl!! Big baby girl. She was over 9 lbs. with a head of hair that a bald man could only wish for. I cleaned the baby off with the help of a couple of brothers. She started crying. I knew that was a great sign!! I told the mother to place the baby next to her chest. I looked at that little girl and was like *wow*!! EMS got to house and complimented us on the nice job. They were getting ready to cut the cord, and the one EMT was a little hesitant, so I took the scalpel, and he clamped the cord and I cut it. Then they wrapped her in a clean blanket and were packing the placenta again. The one EMT hesitated, so I packed it while holding the baby. One of the brothers asked the mother if she had picked out a name. She told them no. The brother said why don't you name her Thelissa? Well what was a joke that turned out to be that little girls name...Thelissa!! The EMT's were going to carry the baby out to the bus (ambulance). I said no!! I delivered her; I will carry her out. The mother got up and walked out like it was another day in the office. *There's that saying again.* When the mother was laying in the bus holding her baby, she said thanks and asked me my name. I gave it to her. We walked back to the rig, and I looked down the block where the night before laid a young man with a bullet hole in his head and watched him breathe his last breath. Today a new life has entered this world by the grace of God; right down the block where pure evil took a life!! By the time we got back to quarters (firehouse) all the people in the neighborhood knew about the baby. They all came over to congratulate us on the delivery. One of the old timers from the neighborhood told me that they will ask you to be the Godfather when the baby gets baptized. He told me not to do it because the family will expect you to support the child. I said what about the father? He just smiled and said, "Which one?" A couple of weeks later the family came to the firehouse to ask me to be the Godfather. Someone forgot to tell me, and when I found out I was not happy because I would have done it with honor. I helped bring her into this world, and I wanted to try and help her out of the violence of the neighborhood in the Bronx. You see I know how to deliver a baby because a few weeks before the baby was born, my son was born and I cut the cord and held him in my arms. A proud moment in my personal life which was full of stress and turmoil, but I was learning to live with this stress and turmoil, not that I liked it. With so much craziness going on daily, both at work and at home, I had no safe place to get away from it all, so I started going to a little church in the Bronx.

Later in the week we had another job late at night. It was an H-type building, and the fire was on the 5th floor. There were calls of children in the apartment. We got up to the fire floor and were assisting the first due company when a family member came up and said a little boy was missing. He was trapped in the back bedroom. Well now all hell breaks out, and we make our way into the apartment when one of the brothers hands me a lifeless body of a little boy. As I carry the little boy, one of the brothers from Rescue 3 starts to give him CPR with oxygen. My officer follows us down the stairs as we are trying to bring life back into this little boy. I prayed a silent prayer the whole time I held him and asked God to spare his life. When we got down to the street, the bus was nowhere around, so the officer from Rescue 3 said we don't have time to wait, get in the rescue rig and let's go! The boy didn't respond to the CPR. I said to myself *Please God! Please, God!! Don't let this little boy die!*! We got about three blocks from the hospital, and he started coughing and getting sick. I held him to the side, and he vomited and kept coughing!! He made it!! *The brother giving the CPR and oxygen was a brother who I worked with when I first got the job. His name was Christopher Blackwell who did an unbelievable job on not giving up on that child! My officer who was working that night name was John Williamson, both of these heroes would die on September 11, 2001. When we gave the boy over to the doctors in the hospital, I thanked God for saving this little boy's life... what a week!!* The death of a young man to the birth of a beautiful baby girl, to the near death of a little boy and getting to see him come back from near death. It had caught up with me. I went to the upstairs of the firehouse and cried happy but sad tears for this little boy. What was reported on the investigation of the fire was that the mother went down to a friend's apartment on the 2nd floor and left the kids alone. The oldest being about 11 years old and this young boy being the youngest at five years old were left in the house when the young boy was playing with matches. A small fire started in the room, and all the kids got out of the apartment, but the little boy was afraid he was going to get in trouble, so he ran back into his room to hide. Thank God the brothers never gave up. You see we don't see the color of people's skin, or the amount in their bank account, or the God they worship or even if they don't like us. We will do anything to save a life, even risk our own to save a stranger.

13

These Things Don't Just Happen... My Guardian Angel!

While my life was crazy at the firehouse, it was just as crazy in my private life, but it seemed that God had everything under control. I just didn't know it. You see I had worked in E-42 for about two years when my uncle had passed away. He was a legend in the sanitation department. His nickname was Downtown, Larry Brown!! He stood about 5'7" weighed about 167 lbs. He was the toughest man I knew besides my father. His claim to fame was that he could roll 5- 55-gallon drums at the same time full of ash from the coal-burning stoves. He also told me he fought the Indians in my backyard upstate where I grew up, and that one of them scalped him. He said that he shined

Babe Ruth shoes after a Yankee game in the Bronx and that the Babe flipped him a silver dollar. That's the one I believe Lol!! He was a great storyteller, but sadly he died from ALS. A sad ending for a great man. I questioned why God would let this happen. Why would he let a proud man get ALS when he always took care of his body? He rode a stationary bike with his legs failing him. He would put his feet in the straps on the pedals and push his legs. He would ride the bike for hours!! I went to see him before he died and made him laugh with the stories he once told me. I gave him a handshake and told him I love him, but I wish I had hugged him and gave him a kiss. See this lesson will come back to me later in my life and career. You have to hold on to the moment because you never know when it will be taken away from you. Well, I needed a couple of days off for the funeral in Brooklyn from the firehouse. I asked the Captain if he could help me out. I said my uncle passed away in Brooklyn, and I needed a couple of days. He told me it was no problem. He said to me, *"You know I knew an Edwards' in Brooklyn"* not knowing my uncle's last name was Lanza. He said this guy was a good friend of mine. His grandmother lived across the street from my house at Park Slope and 7th street, and that his father would take them upstate to visit his grandparents who lived in Stanford, NY. He said his father's name was Charlie, and his mother's name was Marianne and he had a sister named Jackie and he had a little brother who was about two years old before they moved upstate and I never seen him again, but his name was Steve Edwards. Now! All along I am listening to him, and I am saying, "Ok my family is from Brooklyn, my grandmother lives in Stanford, NY! My father's name is Charlie, and that's my mother's name Marianne and I have a sister named Jackie, and damn... my brother's name is Steve, and I was two years old when we moved upstate!! I said, "Cap (nickname for Captain), that's my family!! Steve is my brother!!" He was shocked and said he hadn't seen my brother in over 25 years. I called my brother and told him I have an old friend of his that would like to speak to him. The two of them spoke of old times for about a half an hour. I called my mother and told her and she knew right away. His name was John, and they spoke for a while catching up on family and friends. When I went home, I looked at my family's old pictures, and I found my baptism picture and there he was!! It was a picture of my aunt (holding me) and uncle (Godparents), the priest, my sister and John and my brother as the altar boys. I said these things just don't happen. What are the odds that this would ever happen? It was as if God sent a sign that made me realize that this crazy thing called life is scripted in a good way. Like I was supposed to be there. It made me feel safe, like indestructible. When the brothers saw the picture (you know nothing is sacred in the firehouse), they started teasing the captain. The captain was one of the most respected firefighters and officers on the job. In the 5 1/2 years I worked in E-42, I never heard him raise his voice or curse. We all called him Saint John but I called him my guardian angel. Later on, he would surprise us all with what he said about how the brothers were being treated after September 11, 2001. He is still the greatest FDNY officer I have ever worked with!

14

Keeping it light... Pranks!

The things in the firehouse were getting pretty crazy between the fires and EMS runs in and out. One of the old timer's favorite sayings was, *"We were in and out all night long like a groom on his honeymoon!!" lol!* That's the firehouse humor. There were things that we would laugh at that people on the outside would look at us like we had three heads. Meanwhile, we were doubled over laughing our asses off. You see firehouse humor is a mixture of G, GP, R, and then there is the XXX!! It's all about laughing and knowing that you are working at one of the most dangerous jobs in the world. You would say things and do things to get those laughs. It could be acting out a scene from a movie or speaking the lines of a favorite show, or putting water in someone's boot, having a water fight in the firehouse with the booster hose (a hose connected to the 500-gallon tank in the engine) or pulling a prank on probies. One of the greatest pranks I remember was done to a probie. This young guy comes into the firehouse for his first tour. One of the brothers goes upstairs into the officer's room. We tell the probie that the officer wants to talk to him, meanwhile the brother dresses up like the officer but he has no pants on. The brother is sitting at his desk as the probie comes up to the office. He is all serious and tells the probie to stand at attention and then tells him to turn around, and the brother stands up and he is balls ass naked. The look on the probie's face is priceless. The probie doesn't know whether to run out of the office or stay at attention and meanwhile the brother remains straight-faced. This has happened a few times.

Another great one was when we had a guy named T-Bone (Tommy) who was mildly mentally challenged. He had a job, but loved the firehouse so I would bring him in, and we would watch TV until we had a run. One day a probie was coming in on the night tour, so we dressed T-Bone up as the captain. We had all the brothers sitting at the kitchen table waiting for this kid to come in. When he came in, one of the brothers said the captain wants everybody in the kitchen. He wants to talk to us about drilling. Now, we got T-Bone dressed up as the officer, and he comes walking into the kitchen. The look on the kids face is priceless!! T-Bone walks up to the probie and salutes him and then gives him a hug and kisses his cheek. Now T-Bone starts talking about his favorite cartoon shows as drill and guys keep asking him questions. At this point, we cannot keep a straight face anymore. We all start laughing. The Probie said, "What the hell am I getting into?" T-Bone would come around the firehouse all the time and became part of the FDNY family. He still comes to this day.

There was another Probie who came in a couple of years later. One of the brothers had the probie strip to his underwear. The officer told the brother to check the probie's body for any identifiable marks, just in case something happens to him so they could ID his body. This is one of the greatest pranks!! So in the kitchen with the brothers sitting at the table, this kid takes off his shirt and pants in front of the brother. He asks, "Can I keep my underwear on?" The brother says, "For now you can." He walks around, the probie looking at tattoos and birthmarks and he is writing them all down. Now he says to the probie, "You have to drop your underwear." The probie says, "I have to?" The brother says, "What happens if that's the only thing left of you?" So he drops his draws and is standing completely naked except for his shorts down around his feet. All the brothers are telling him the new captain has ordered all firefighters to go through this (bullshit). Now the brother sees a shamrock tattoo on the probie's ass. He writes it down then he says, "Ok, pull them up." The probie bends down to pull up his shorts and the brother says, "What are you doing?" Probie says, "Well you told me to pull them up!" The brother says, "Not your shorts, your ball bag"!! Now the whole room is roaring, rolling on the floor! This kid was the greatest!!

Then there was one night when a brother brought in Rocky Horror Picture Show, the movie. Well, this brother was a painter and on the side he would do big jobs like houses. This night he brings in a bag of rags that his wife's friend gave her. We get a job about two hours into the tour. We knock the fire down (put it out) and then head back to quarters (firehouse). We stop to get dinner. While we pick up dinner, we get hot dogs and bread and water guns. You see Rocky Horror Picture Show is a movie you have to participate in. So when the movie starts, you throw toast at one another, or you get sprayed with water or get hit with a hot dog. Yes, a hot dog!! lol! Well, the brother goes into his bag of rags and finds women's dresses, all sizes, and colors. As we are getting cleaned up, he walks into the kitchen dressed in this great dress. We start laughing our asses off. Now he puts on the movie. Then another brother goes out and comes back in with a dress on. He brings in the bag of dresses, and we all put them on and are watching the movie, spraying one another with water, toast flying around and

91

getting hit in the head with a flying hot dog. We are all laughing our asses off. You see the only problem was that we had a few runs in between where we had to wear the dresses under our turnout gear. Thank God we didn't have anything big (fire). We also had a covering officer. This is an officer from another company somewhere in the city. The lieutenant had no idea about the movie and the dresses in the kitchen. When we get back in, we all take off our turnout gear and walk in the back with these dresses on. He doesn't blink an eye. He walks upstairs and closes the door to the office. We go back in and put the movie back on and start throwing the toast and hot dogs around, and the water is flying all over. Next thing you know the door opens up and it's the covering lieutenant in a beautiful red gown. We all start laughing, and he says, "You weren't going to invite me?" Well, he sat down with a water gun and toast, and hot dogs were flying again. He said, "This is the greatest! I have never been in a house with such crazy guys but when the shit hit the fan (Fire) ... You guys are the greatest!"

You see in busy houses you have to keep things light because you never know what might happen to you at the next job. These were the greatest of times. We would have guys stand outside, and someone on the roof would have a pail of water waiting for someone to walk into the target zone and get drenched by this bucket of water. We would bet a brother that he cannot climb the pole from the first floor to the second, and then when he is half way up, hit him with a bag of flour!! The rule of engagement is never damage anyone's personal property or fire equipment. These were off limits, but some guys just didn't understand, and it caused some fights. One time one of these brothers (who just didn't get it) took plumber cement and glued my locker shut. Well, I went crazy because he had done things like this to others in the firehouse. He would push things way too far, and I had it. I went down to the truck and got an ax and was heading up to his locker to hack it up!! Some of the brothers talked sense into me and told me to put the ax down, and I did. I called the brother up at home and told him, "*Wait till I see*

93

you tomorrow, you and I are going to go at it, this BS has to stop all the brothers are tired of your act." The next morning when he came in all the brothers were waiting around the kitchen for the fireworks. He came in with a bag of rolls and cake in his arms and said, "Can I talk to you outside?", and I said, "Let's go!" When we got out there, he said in all my years on the job I've always looked forward to coming into work but today I didn't want to come to face you. We had a good talk, and I said, "You push things to a point where it becomes personal, and you have to know the rules of engagement. You don't fuck with the brother's personal property when we play around in the firehouse." Then he started to enlarge a picture of the brothers and started putting them on magazine covers or crazy pictures with their faces on the bodies of people in the news. You see I created a monster. Now that's funny!

One day the officer in the engine got hurt at a job, and the senior man had to take over for the officer. Well, I was the senior man, and I got the seat (to be the officer of the rest of the tour).

94

Well at about 10 am I get a call from the Buildings Department telling me that we had a complaint in our area for an illegal daycare center. Which means we have to check on this complaint. I ask the officer in the truck what we have to look for? He tells me to make sure there are no more than five children and that they are of the same family. Check the apartment out for anything that would make you think it might be a daycare. Ok, now we have the address and are pulling up to the building down the road from the firehouse. We get up and I knock and an old women answers. I ID myself and explain the complaint and she says, "These 6 kids are her grandchildren." I looked around and there was no signs of a daycare, so I told her, *No problem nothing to worry about*." We go back to quarters and I tell the truck officer what I seen and he said fills out the paperwork with "unfounded." About an hour later I get another phone call. I answer the call, and the guy ID's himself as a building inspector from headquarters and he says, "Officer Edwards, I'm sorry I gave you the wrong apartment number. I said, "Are you sure this time?" "Yes, this is the number, same

address but a different apartment number."
Now I speak to the truck officer again and I
explain what happened, and he told me I had to
go check it out. The house Watchmen turns out
the engine again. The guys are pissed. We go
back to the same building and go to a different
apt number. I knock on the door little girl
answers, and I identify myself and ask to speak
to a parent. She says, "My dad is sleeping, he
works nights." I said, "You have to get dad up; I
have to speak to him." She goes into a room,
and I look around, and there are no signs of a
daycare. Now the father comes to the door and
says, "What's the problem?" I tell him the story
about the complaint and he goes crazy!! "Who
called up?" "Is it the fuck downstairs?" Now he
is banging his foot on the floor cursing and
screaming. I tell him to calm down. He says the
asshole has been complaining all the time about
my children. "Relax," I said, "There is nothing
that makes your apartment a daycare. He says,
"I'm going to kill the bastard one day!!" I told
him again, "Don't worry about it." Now we
head back to quarters again. I go back to talk to
the truck officer again. I told him I think we
might have a murder on our hands because that

guy wants to kill his neighbor who he thinks called the complaint on him. By now we are all pissed! Well just when you think it's safe, the Building Inspector calls me again. This time apologizing to me about the whole thing and that someone gave him the wrong address, and that's it's the building on the other side of the block but to be careful because there is a drug den in this building near the complaint apartment. Now I ask this guy, *"Are you sure!!? "This is the third time you have us going out, and it's getting kind of crazy!!* The guy says, "No, no this is it." So we turn out again. The brothers are bitching and complaining. We get to the building, and I tell the chauffeur to call for police backup. The dispatcher called back and said that he doesn't know anything about this complaint or about having police backup. I am pissed. I tell the brothers to wait downstairs in the lobby while I check on this daycare bullshit! They say we are not leaving you alone at the door with a possible drug den nearby. So a couple of the brothers waited next to the stairwell as I knocked on the door. I screamed, *"Fire Dept.!!"* No answer! Again I screamed, *"Fire Dept!"* Again no answer, but I hear people running around in the apartment. I radio to the chauffeur to tell them that it's unfounded. Now we all get back in the rig (engine), and we are cursing up a storm calling that building guy every name in the book!! We turn the corner heading to the firehouse, and I see all the brothers out in the street laughing their heads off doubled over, and some were crying from laughing so hard!! You see *I had been pranked!!* I went over to the truck officer, and he was crying. He said you looked so official I could not stop you!! I had to laugh because remember you never let them see something bothers you and don't let them know that they got to you!! I asked some of the great pranksters in the house, but no one confessed. Later on in the years I found out who it was. A great comedian of the firehouse had gotten me good! What happened to him a few years later would bring tears of sadness to my eyes!

15

The End of a Great Run in E42

 My career at E42 was coming to an end. I just felt that there were more reasons to transfer out to another firehouse. After five years working in E42, I learned and seen so much in that house. The great guys I worked with who will be family for life were priceless. You see things were pointing me back to the house I originally came from, but the memories of E42 would live with me forever, and people I meet along the way will always hold a special place in my heart. I remember one night at a job across from Cortona Park, there was a fire on the top floor, and the roof had holes in it, exposing the stars and the dark of night. Only the full moon's glow shined through the holes in the roof and the hollowed out windows. One of the brothers called me into the living room /kitchen area where the front window was burnt out, and the red bricks of the exterior wall were showing. There was smoke from burnt wood and steam that was rising from the bricks from the burnt-out window frames, exposing the full moon. I swear if it was possible, it looked like you could reach out and touch it because it felt like you could see all the craters. I looked into the kitchen, and there was water flowing out of a broken pipe in the kitchen sink. It all seemed so surreal, all these effects happening around this room as the full moon peaked in the window. I will never forget that night.

Another one of my favorite moments was working on New Year's Eve. We had bought a nice meal for this night. There was a crew working seven days a week, 365 days a year, and 24 hours a day in every firehouse in the city. We don't get off for holidays. We work on weekends. We work on our kid's birthdays. This is just the way it is. You could get off if someone would work for you, but you have to pay him back and work one of his tours (shifts). So this

New Year's Eve was planned out to be a nice night spending it with the brothers, my second family, but around 10 pm we get a run (fire) to a vacation warehouse. This fire was roaring through the roof of this giant warehouse. The flames are twenty feet above the roof. The fire went to a 2nd Alarm. We had five engines, two ladder companies, two battalion chiefs, rescue companies, one satellite unit (special unit) there must have been a total of 75 firefighters on the roof and around the warehouse. It was a total loss that would later be labeled suspicious. We were keeping the fire from extending to other buildings. The one building next to this warehouse was the 52 Precinct on Webster Ave. It was a cold night. The only thing keeping us warm was the fire. We were on a roof of another warehouse throwing water on the fire as the ball was ready to drop. The only way we knew this was there was a window in the precinct that we could see the clock on the wall. So when there was a minute left we all started counting down for the New Year 10,9,8,7,6,5,4,3,2,1...*Happy New Year we all screamed!!!!* We hugged one another, and there were brothers singing Auld Lang Syne!!

See what we did was have one of the best New Year's we possibly could with our second family! Hey! How many people can say they spent New Year's celebrating with the greatest bunch of guys on earth while fighting the largest warehouse fire, and praying for a better year all around, personally, professionally, and spiritually? We worked the fire till 4 am just in time for the fire to go out and realize it was getting cold. When we got back to the firehouse, we cleaned up and had another fire that morning. What a way to start off a New Year. *Action!!*

Some of the greatest things in life just happen! These are the memories that you never want to let go of or have fade. See E42 was full of some of the greatest characters, just brothers being themselves was a laugh. One morning we get a run up to an area in the Bronx, the Belmont section known as Arthur Ave also known as Little Italy. The streets are full of Italian restaurants, pizza parlors, bakeries, pastry shop, butcher shops and fresh seafood stores. Then you have the Arthur Ave Market, a place to shop when you cannot walk on the street because of rain or bad weather. It's an inside market all owned by families that have been there for years. My favorite is called Cafe Al Mercato. A family owned restaurant, where the father watches over the tables and the register, and their mom cleans off the tables. It started off with three brothers, the Esposito family, now there is one brother left with a great staff of cooks and pizza makers. On this day... it was too early to stop in and bring back breakfast to the firehouse, so on the way back from the run we figured we could pick up lunch and breakfast at the same time. The smell of fresh baked bread flooded the streets and we decided to pick some up. Because it's too far away from quarters to be able to shop there everyday, we figured this was a chance to get good food. The grocery stores in our area had different types of food. You see the stores in neighborhoods cater to the people living in it. So in the stores in our response area you could put every animal back together. They never wasted any part of the animal, every part of the chicken from the head to the feet, every part of a cow inside and out, all of the goat! It was tough shopping unless you knew how to cook chicken feet... lol So we convinced the officer to stop the rig and run in and get two dozen fresh baked Arthur Ave Rolls!! It would be a big treat for the brothers! As we come out of the bakery we get another run back to the same call for an odor of smoke. We just get on the rig and back we go before we realize it's another 10-92 (false alarm). Now we are heading back to quarters when one of the brothers, Bada Bing, asks if we have butter in the refrigerator. I tell him no. He calls up to the officer and asks him, "Hey Lou we need butter for the rolls." The boss was in a bit of a rush to get back. He had paperwork to send into the battalion. He turns around and shouts back, "We have to get back to quarters!!" Bada Bing screams, "We are going by a store at the light. It will take a minute!" The officer screams back at him, "No!! I have to get back!!" Next thing we know Baba Bing takes the bag moist from the steam coming off those hot Arthur Ave Rolls, and as we are on Webster Ave says "Then here are your fucking rolls!!", and throws the bag out the window! The officer screams, "No!!!!!" As I look out the window, like a man who just lost the winning ticket to the lotto, I see two dozen hot rolls rolling around Webster Ave. At first we started asking him what the hell did you do that for? He said, *"If he cannot stop for butter then he cannot have any fucking rolls!!"* At the time it happened we were all in shock!! But as the day went on, the jokes started to roll out (no pun intended). I told Bada Bing I seen a homeless guy on his knees praying to God to give him some food for the day. Next thing he knows he gets hit with two dozen hot rolls flying through the air hitting him on the head as he picks up the rolls thanking God! To this day every time I see or speak to Bada Bing or any of the brothers we laugh our asses off about that day. See these are the memories we never want to let go of. These are the things that just happen and leave great memories that we still laugh about 25 years later!!

There was another job we had where I was working in a truck company, and it was freezing. The wind was blowing so hard that the snow was coming down sideways. It was another big job, a mansion was on fire in Riverdale in the

Bronx, and the fire destroyed the whole inside of the home. I was in a tower ladder (has a bucket with a nozzle that puts out a lot of water for big jobs). The brothers in the truck were trying to figure out who was going to get in the bucket. I told them I'd go, and another brother stepped up. In the bucket we went. It was cold on the way up, but when we raised it up to the side of the building it was warm and hot. I started throwing water on the far side of the building. The brother asked me why I was hitting the fire on the other side and not near us. I asked him if he would you rather freeze up here. He laughed. I explained to him hitting the fire on the far side keeps us warm. We spent two hours in the bucket! We had to open our turnout coats because we were sweating. At one point, the officer told use to come down and take a break, and I told him we were good. I looked down they were huddled around the exhaust from the truck to stay warm. This is why I always stepped up on all the jobs because of what I had learned from the best. *Experience is the best teacher!*

16

Saying Goodbye to My Hero... My Dad

I was torn between staying at E42 and transferring to my original company, but something happened that just pushed me over the edge. My father passed away when I was at E42. My father was my hero as a kid growing up. I knew about him fighting in the Battle of the Bulge in World War II. He also was a NYC Sanitation Police Officer. He carried a gun and rode a scooter. He would give out tickets for littering when the city really cared about those things. He had to shoot a man who stabbed his wife on the city streets. He was not tall or muscular. He was pound for pound one of the toughest men I know. He was a great role model to me and my family. He was tough both inside and out. My father was not a complainer, but he was having hip pain. The doctor was telling him and my family that he had arthritis of the hip, but after further testing we found out it was cancer. I was devastated. I had the job of rescuing people. Now this time it was my father. I had to be there with him every step of the way. The brothers in the firehouse were great. The job was unbelievable. I called up and told headquarters about my father being terminally ill with cancer. They told me to check in every week and speak to someone at the medical office to make sure they had an update on how he was doing. We took my father all over, starting at Sloan Kettering. When we were there, the doctor told him he could treat him with chemo and replace his hip, but could not promise that he could get better. I walked out into the hall for a moment to gather myself. My mother waited with my father, my cousin and Dave. Yes, that's right the guy who busted my father's balls all these years was there to support my dad and my family. You see you can change. As I was in the hallway of the hospital, I looked down the hall and seen a familiar face. It was Coach Jimmy Valvano, the coach who led North Carolina State to its 1983 National

Championship in Basketball. He was standing next to his wife, and I went over to him and introduced myself and told him I was a NYC Firefighter and a big fan and that I was praying for him. He thanked me and asked what I was in the hospital for. I told him it was my father and that he had bone cancer. Coach Valvano said, *"Hey listen, me and your dad are going to beat cancer!"* I shook his hand and wished him well and told him I will keep him in my prayers. I walked away with hope that this could come true, but it didn't for both Coach V and my dad. After hearing that they really had no good news for us, we took my dad to Westchester to see another doctor who really had no bedside manners. He came out and told my dad there was nothing he could do for him, and he would make him comfortable. *I wanted to knock this guy out! Make him comfortable? We are here to make him well again!* I think when my dad heard this it took the fight out of him. Now I had been out of work for two weeks at the time. I had to call FDNY headquarters to check in and spoke to one of the brothers, and I told him that it was just a matter of time. He asked how long it was going to take. I said, *"What?"* He said,

"You have been out for two weeks?" *How long is he going to hold on for?* Remember about the 1% of bad brothers? Well here is one of them. I jumped all over this guy on the phone and told him if I ever run into him he better keep his distance because he will regret his words! I hung up the phone. I was in shock! How could anybody say this to anyone? I called the firehouse and told the captain (my guardian angel). He called up headquarters and told the brother (I use that term loosely to describe that low life) off! The Westchester doctor gave my father pain meds, heavy duty pain medicine. He was not sleeping at night. He would hold onto the side of the bed sitting up. It was tough seeing him in such pain, but I gained even more respect for him-- if that was possible to do. I went with my brother to pick up the pain medicine at the pharmacy, and they told us that this is very powerful medicine. Watch him when he takes it. He took the first pill and tried to sleep and he couldn't. We gave him the second pill in the morning, and he was sitting in the wheelchair. We put him under the peach tree in the backyard, and it looked like he was falling asleep. Later that night I went to the gym and

got a phone call from home telling me that my father had to be rushed to the hospital, something was wrong with him. I got home I ran into the house to see my father in the wheelchair. His skin was cold, and he was turning blue. See, as firefighters we were really never trained on what to look for at the time this happened to my dad, but like the old saying goes, *If I only knew now what I didn't know then, I might have been able to save my dad.* I know you are probably saying he would have suffered, this is true, but I miss him. A couple of years later we were trained, and I know what happened to my dad. The ambulance shows up, and my dad is non-responsive. We go to take him out of the wheelchair, and he grabbed the wheelchair like he didn't want to leave the house. My mother tells me to ride with my dad in the ambulance. They put him in, and he is lifeless. I start telling him, *"Dad hold on! Dad don't do this to me." "I don't want to tell mom!!" Hold on!! Please!* We got up to the hospital and rushed him in, and the doctor gave him a shot. I didn't know what it was then, but found out later. It is called Naloxone or Narcan as it's called, is an antidote to opioid drugs.

opioids can slow or stop a person's breathing, which causes death. Well little did I know that when this is given to patients, they come out of it, but then they go right back to that level after it wears off. When we left the hospital that night, my father was sitting up speaking to us in a low voice. The doctor told us to come back in the morning. We all gave my father a kiss. The next morning, I called headquarters and told them about my father being rushed and admitted to the hospital. The brother told me good luck with your dad. I will be praying for him. This brother was the 99.9% of the great guys on the job. Well thinking that we would see my father better this morning and feeling better about calling into the FDNY -- we get a phone call from the hospital. They said to bring up a priest and you might want to sign a DNR (do-not-resuscitate). My brother and I went up to the hospital, and my uncle brought the priest. My father was hooked up to all these machines. *Here is my hero... the man I looked up to laying in front of me motionless. The hands I used to hold as a child were cold and pale. I gave him a kiss.* My brother, who went through the Vietnam War, and who never really shows emotions walked outside the room after praying for my father. The priest came in and leaned over my father to give him the last rights. My father reached up and hugged the priest! We couldn't believe what my dad just did. I started crying and walked outside the room. See my dad was not a very religious man. He believed in God, but didn't go to church much. Now it was like he was accepting God into his heart. All our family members came up to say goodbye. My father went into the hospital on the 28th of July and held on to see all six grandkids, including my son who was the the last one to say good-bye. He had been visiting his mom down in Florida and flew up a week early when he heard about his grandfather. It was a Friday night and my dad was laying there still hooked up to the respirator that was breathing for him. He was in a heavily sedated state. My son came in and leaned over my father, and he reached up and hugged my son. There wasn't a dry eye in the room. My son being the last grandchild my father waited to see. My mother and brother and I stayed there till 6am. My brother wanted my mother to get some sleep. We all said goodbye again and kissed and hugged him and left, all along expecting to see him get better. We got home and my brother went back up and my mother went to bed, and I had to drive my girlfriend back to work. I dropped her off and started to head back home. I took the George Washington Bridge up route 4 heading north to Route 17 North. All of a sudden, I get this chill that runs throughout my body, and I start to cry. I felt as if something bad had happened like my father had died. It was an uncontrollable cry, as I turn on the radio to change the mood, I notice the clock and it read 8:47 am and a song comes on *"Somewhere out There."* Now I cannot pull myself together. I cried all the way to my house a 45 minute drive. I pulled up to the house. I didn't see my brother's car in the driveway. I said, "Thank God. It was just a bad feeling." I ran into my mother's bedroom, and she was asleep. I went out the back door to head up to the hospital to be with my father. My brother pulled up in the driveway! I went over to him and asked, "Dad died?" He shook his head and said, "Yes." Well I told him my story about the feeling and the song and the time and he said, "Dad died at 9:00 am." We hugged and I said, "I want to go up and see

114

him." We went in and told my mother and passed the word throughout the family. Before we made the arrangements, I called the hospital and told them that I wanted to see my father and say goodbye to him. The hospital said he was in the hospital morgue. I told them I was a NYC Firefighter, and they said ok. I went up with my brother, and they took my father's body out. He was wrapped in the same sheet he died in, and they left me there with him. His eyes were open. *I took my hand and closed them. I held his hand like I was a child again and hugged him and cried. I thanked him for all he had given me and I apologized for all the times we argued. I told him that I loved him and that I will miss him and that he should never worry about my mother because I would take care of her. I spent 15 minutes with my hero, my role model, my friend, MY FATHER!* At my dad's funeral, all the brothers from different firehouses came to the wake and the funeral. There were a hundred people coming to pay their respects. I thought I knew everything about my dad, till those few days. People came up to me and told me stories that I had never heard. They told me how he helped people out when they were in trouble

and how proud he was I was a NYC Firefighter.
Thanks, Pop, till we meet again, I love you!

17

An Accident, a Miracle, and My Guardian Angels

Coming back to work after my father died was tough. Even though the job was a great release of tension and frustration, the loss was very tough to handle at times. I remember the feeling I had driving home. The messages were everything to me, that all the death I seen in the last 10 years, that there was a place for these victims' souls. I felt my father gave me the answer. I started to take risks not with the brother's lives but with my own. I remember being detailed (filling manpower at another firehouse) to a truck company and I had the roof. The first due roofman has to take a route to the opposite stairwell to the roof of the fire building. The second due roofman had to take a different route than the first due. I was the second due roofman. We pulled up to the building, and I sized up the job and the building. I knew that the only way up to the roof was from the building alongside of the job. I ran up the stairs and got to the roof and seen that there was a three foot difference from the front of the building to the back. I took off my gear and tied a rope to it and seen if I got up on the ledge of the building I could hoist myself up to the other roof and pull up my gear with the rope. This was not in the books. The chief and the job would have gone nuts if they saw the danger I put myself in. I climbed on the parapet wall and grabbed onto to the fire buildings parapet and pulled myself over. *One slip and I fall six stories down to an alley.* I spoke to my father and said, *"Pop be with me!"* And over I went! I got up to the roof and pulled my gear up and looked and saw the first due roof man didn't make it up yet. I started to vent by opening up the bulkhead door and taking the vent off of the roof to give the brothers a break from all the smoke. The roofman's job is to vent the building. By venting the building, the smoke lifts and heads up the stairwells. This is why they tell you never go up to the roof in case of a fire, always use the stairs below the fire or another stairwell on the opposite side of the fire floor. We have found some people dead near the bulkhead door or in the stairwell above the fire floor. They die from smoke inhalation. When the brother got up to the roof, he was shocked to see me and that I had vented to roof. He said, "How the fuck did you get up here so fast"? I told him the other building. He walked over and looked down and said, "You climbed up on the ledge of the Parapet?" I asked him if he really wanted to know. He shook his head and smiled and said, "Chris, you must have a guardian Angel!" I said, "Yes I do!" After I came off the roof, the chief told me it was a nice job and asked how I got up there so fast. I told him, but never said a word about the ledge walk. Lol! The messages I got from my father were real!

One night coming back from a retirement party for one of the brothers, I was driving on the Palisades Parkway. It was late, and I had just got finished working a 24-hour shift and then the

119

party. I was tired. I started to fall asleep driving. I pulled over a few times, and thought I felt good enough; I had to get home. Finally, I pulled over one last time, and I closed my eyes and jumped up thinking I was still driving, but I was parked. It was the shot of adrenaline!! I grabbed the wheel and said, "I feel great." I drove a few more miles and then I fell asleep again. I looked up and a deer ran across the road. Ahead of me was a fork in the road and I couldn't correct myself and went directly into the exit sign. The sign took out the windshield and through the woods I went. I remember the trees hitting the side of the car. It sounded like a baseball card attached to the spoke of a bicycle wheel. Finally, the car came to a sudden stop. Bang!! Now it's 2:30 am. I am about forty feet into the woods of trees and rocks. I turn to the back seat and say, "Are you all right?" Then I realized I was alone. I had taken my belt off when I laid down that last stop. I go to open the door and realize I am sitting on the driver's side door. The car had flipped on its side, a perfect landing. I climbed out the passenger side window. I make my way to the trees and try and wave someone down, but two people passed. I know that I had to turn the headlights on so I went back in the woods and climbed back into the car and turned the lights on. Now I walk to the other side of the road and wave a car down. The guys asked if the people were alright. I told him I was the only one in the car. He was surprised I made it out alive. He went into town and called an ambulance and then another car stopped. It couldn't have been any better. He was an EMT from the FDNY. He took care of me and I told him I was fine. He looked at me and said, *"It is a miracle you didn't get hurt"* I was fine just felt a little sick. The next car was another EMT from the FDNY. This was like the perfect rescue. Then the state police showed up and asked me what happen, and I told them about the deer and I couldn't correct myself and hit the sign. They were amazed on how I got out of the car. I went to the hospital and was released within an hour. No injuries, just a small inch, and a half scratch under my eye. I went home and got some sleep and in the morning went up to get my things from the car. After my father passed away, I carried his picture and my uncle's mass card with me on the dashboard. My son and I went up and picked up my belongings from the junkyard, but there was just one problem. My father's picture and my Uncle's mass card were missing. So we took a ride to the accident site and wow! I was lucky. To see it in the daytime was scary. I missed a big tree by a foot, and to see where the car came to a stop on top of a pile of rocks surrounded by trees and grass and a pond about 50 feet away, was nothing short of a miracle. My son and I walked around, and I found my uncle's mass card. We couldn't find my father's picture. We walked around for about an hour in the woods looking for his picture and couldn't find it. It was in January, and it was cold and windy. So I was upset about not finding it, but as we walked out of the woods, my son seen something on top of this frozen pond about half way out. It was next to a lump of grass sticking out of the ice. I walked out on the frozen pond, and there it was, my father's picture clinging to a blade of grass. I started to get emotional because I remember having that feeling and looking to the back seat and saying *"Are you all right?"* My father and uncle were with me the whole time. After all these things happened, I started to go to church every Sunday and I would stop by a little church in the Bronx, St. Lucy. It has a beautiful grotto outside with a waterfall of holy water. This was the beginning of my journey. I started to pray for all the friends and family that had passed away since I was a child. I figured if my father can show me he was in a better place, I should keep them all alive in my heart and soul, so I started saying a prayer for about ten friends and loved ones. By the time the FDNY retired me, the number of people I would pray for had grown to an unbelievable amount of loss.

18

Search, Rescue, and Adrenaline

The feeling of being indestructible was a good feeling, but it was a bad thing to have as a firefighter because the red devil (fire) always wins in the end one way or another. You see the fire department went out and supplied us with new gear. The old gear was a turnout coat, jeans, a helmet that weighed about three pounds, fireproof gloves and a pair of thigh-high rubber boots that you would pull up before you went into a fire to protect your knees from being burnt. It really didn't do much for your thighs if hot water hit your jeans. We were later issued bunker gear; this was a two-piece uniform made up of a turnout coat and bunker pants with, yes, red suspenders and a hood meant to keep your face from getting burnt.

The problem is that you go in further then we need to be. We had a job, and I was working in a truck that day. Crawling down the hall, I found the fire in the back room. I opened the door, and it was a bedroom fully charged (fire and smoke). I crawled into the room and was doing a search. I really couldn't stand up. I swept (search) the bed and checked under it. It was clear. I made my way to the closet and opened the door. I go towards the door to get out, and the radio calls that the line is in position near the bedroom door, and it is charged (water on). I screamed to the engine to hold up till I got out. I raised up to my knees and turned and made my way out. When I got out to the hallway, the officer asked me how I got in the room and told me I had done a good job in the search, but if you see a room with that much fire, there's a chance that the person would be a roast. We went into the kitchen where we had to shut the gas off to the stove. I turned on the flashlight on my helmet. It wasn't working. One of the brothers turns and said, *"Holy shit!! Your flashlight is melted!!"* I took it off and it had melted to my helmet. It was so hot in that room that when I raised up to turn around that's all it took. The heat was that intense. The paint on my helmet was peeled off and burnt on the front piece (badge number and House number ID). When we had the old gear you would feel the heat and you would back out, but with this gear you feel a lot less heat, and that's what gets you burnt. The brothers were impressed that I got in that far and didn't get burnt. They were all laughing, and guys came over to me and congratulated me on a nice job.   The feeling that nothing can happen to me would be a false feeling of security...This feeling of being indestructible would play a big part in my career.

I thought I would be able to work 30 years on the job like I planned, but for the amount of stress and physical abuse you go through just getting ready to get on the rig is a lot. I am not even talking about pulling up to the job (fire). You carry about 75 pounds in equipment on your back and shoulders. Then you have your tools that adds another 20 pounds. You run up to the fire building sizing it up, looking where the smoke or fire is coming from; what room, which wing of the building, looking for people on the fire escape or people at windows. Every brother is sizing up the job as we pull in, things like where to go, how to get there (roofman), what tools will I need, but that goes for everyone. So the stress of getting on the rig, to pulling up to the scene-- the mental stress begins. The physical part is getting to the spot you are assigned to be at, be it... the roof, outside ventman, irons man, canman, officer. Hopefully, you don't have a screamer for an officer (panics a little...lol). The chauffeur even has stress to find a hydrant that works and make sure there is no car parked in front of it. That's when he has to try and get the line hooked up to the engine to supply the engine company with water (charge the line). The weather conditions, freezing, cold, heat, darkness, all these things play into effect of the stress of the job as well as getting people out of the building and rescuing them. The most important is making it home to your family.

We had a job one day. It was a top floor fire, and we had to go do a search in the other wing of an H-type building. When we got to the 6th floor, there was a woman she was burnt from her head down to her waist. She was in shock. Standing next to neighbors, her skin was peeling off her arms but she was not screaming. The officer called to the chief and asked for EMS to come up and help her, but they were waiting for another bus (ambulance) to come in. The officer said we have to get her downstairs. I told him I would take her. We started to walk near the stairs; she could not take it. So I grabbed her around the waist and put her over my shoulder and with all my gear on I ran down six flights of stairs and then ran about 50 yards to an ambulance. I put her down, and the EMT'S took over. She thanked me in Spanish. I told her no problem, but when I stopped to go back upstairs, both knees started to burn with pain. Then I just realized what I had done. I carried a woman that weighed about 125 lbs., 6 flights of stairs and sprinted 50 yards with about 65 pounds of equipment on my shoulder. For a second, I wanted to take that break and sit down for a moment, but I couldn't I had my brothers working shorthanded doing the search. I started to jog back up the stairs and finished the search. You see when that adrenalin kicks in you can do anything... No pain, no gain, never give up mentality!

19

Second Job, New Probie and Strange Coincidences

It had been a few months since my dad died and I was still dragging a heavy heart. You see my kids were living with my mom and dad and they were very close to my parents. My father passing really put stress on the whole family. My mother was mourning and so were my son and daughter. Going to work with this on my mind really made things difficult because your mind is not on the job. That makes every call dangerous. You see there were enough distractions, but they weren't working. The firehouses have sport teams that we play other firehouses in the Bronx all summer long. We were coming around to the playoffs and we would play double headers one day a week and after the game all the firehouses playing on that day would stick around and have a BBQ. It was a little bit of a break, but even then I wasn't myself. We struggled to make it to the playoffs and ended up losing in the Bronx finals. At the BBQ, one of the brothers from the house comes over to me. He had a few beers, and I guess he was trying to help me deal with my fathers' death. He said, "When are you going to get over it?" I said, *"What!!!" I hope it never happens to you, but I will ask you when it does!"* Right then and there I realized it was time to transfer out. A senior man from E81 came over to me and said, "Chris are you ready to come home back to E81?" I had never thought about it till he said it to me. I mean, I loved working in E42, but after what the brother said about my father and the white German Shepard ... *Click,* that was just too much to take at times. I told the senior man I would think about it. I thanked him for wanting me back. By this time, I had worked about five years in E42. I was going to miss some of the brothers, the kids on the block, the fires, but at this time my third son was born in 1995 and working in the neighborhood near their house made it a little easier, but before I left the great times continued. There were great guys in that house that would later transfer to other companies in the Bronx and Manhattan, others would retire after September 11, 2001, but the great memories of those crazy times will live with me and have made me the person I am today.

The movie *Goodfellas* was watched in the firehouse almost every day. We would say the lines to each other all the time. We would reenact all the parts. It was a laugh a minute when you had the right guys around. It seemed like all of the Martin Scorsese movies, *Casino, Goodfellas* and even the movie *The Bad Lieutenant.* Before I left E-42, I started a second job that people beg to have. One day I was getting off of work when one of the brothers called the firehouse looking for two firefighters to be in a movie that was being shot down in Manhattan. I spoke to him, and he said they were shooting a movie in a Washington Heights school, and needed two firefighters for the movie. So one of the brothers getting off work said we should do it, but the only thing was we needed a suit so I went to one of the neighbors and asked her if her husband had a suit we could borrow. She came out with two suits, and we were off to make a movie. When we got to the holding area at the school, there was like a hundred people sitting around waiting to be called up to the scene of the movie. The movie was *Die Hard with a Vengeance*. We had to report into the head casting guy, and he asks us if we were bomb squad experts. I said, "No, we are firemen." He said, "I am sorry I need bomb squad detectives." So we turned to walk away he says, "Guys, come back, if anyone asks, you are bomb squad detectives." Now I was taking a step into a new career, a second job. Well to say the day went well is a story in and of itself. We sat down and waited and waited and waited, and then a guy comes in the room and asks for the two bomb squad detectives not thinking anything about it, we sat there. The guy comes in again and says, "Where are the two bomb squad detectives?!" We didn't even think about what the other guy told us about being bomb squad detectives. Finally, the guy came in and said, "Where is Chris Edwards and Whitey Hyde?" I said, "Damn that's us!!" We jumped up and went over to the AD (assistant director) introduced ourselves and off we went to a room set up to look for a bomb in a school basement. He introduced us to the second team (camera crew) shooting a scene in the basement. The director asks us what we would do if we were looking for a bomb. I thought to myself... what the hell am I going to say? I thought about a movie I had seen and told the director to shut off all two-way radios, and we should use hand signals. He said that was great!! I have no idea on what to do with bombs, but that's why they call it acting. That was the beginning. I ended up working three more weeks on that movie in different scenes. When I got my check, it was about 2500 dollars for a side job. What a big help and I was having fun doing it. The brothers were happy to step up and cover any tours that I needed off. One of the brothers told me I should save the money and forget about joining the union. He said, "You will never work in movies again." That's just what I needed to hear. I joined the union and my second job had just begun. Perfect timing!

I can honestly say I have worked in some of the greatest firehouses during my career and with the greatest group of firefighters who to this day I call my brothers. I transferred back to E-81. There was a new group of guys working now. A lot of the old timers had either retired or transferred out of the house. The brothers that were there now were guys that got on the job with me. The officers had changed, and some real characters had transferred in. It was a young house, with the average age being about 32 years old. Some of the brothers came from busy firehouses throughout the city. What happens is when a brother buys a house upstate, they look to drive a shorter distance which would be the Bronx. So if you were working in Manhattan, you would live in Queens or Staten Island. If you worked in Brooklyn, you might live in Brooklyn, Queens, Staten Island or Long Island. Plus, it depends on how busy you want to be, but for the most part if you had children you would move them out to the suburbs. I ended up buying a house up-state and moved my sons into a house that was about an hour and a half drive to give them a better life. We had a great group of firefighters, but also a great group of athletes. We had guys who were college basketball players, baseball players, swimmers, water polo, football players, and college wrestlers. It was an amazing group of guys. Then we had guys that would make you laugh all night while you ran your ass off fighting fires and other emergencies. It was a great mix of personalities. We had some students (brothers studying to become an officer). I felt coming into E81 was great after learning so much from E42, I could be a big help with the young guys now since I would be a senior man. I would take the probie under my wing and show him the ropes. I would also run them through the initiation. All the probies were great guys that would later play a big part in all of our lives in the house. Some of them were coming through on a rotation system that the city worked out. The probies who have to go to an A, B or C firehouse. These were based on runs for the year and workers (fires). We had some great kids come to work. We had a young guy about 28 years old who came over from the sanitation department. He was a great kid. Then we had guys come over from the NYPD another stand-up guy (do the right thing). We had others coming through on the rotation system from firehouses in Brooklyn, Queens, Manhattan and Staten Island. One of the probies was assigned to the house from Probie School. In a strange way, I heard about him before he came to the firehouse. I was playing in a softball tournament in Georgia. I never played with this team before. I only knew a handful of guys on the team. We flew down to Georgia. I met this guy who was a firefighter in IBM. We hung out all weekend. He said he heard I was a New York City Firefighter and that he knew a guy that just got on the job, but he didn't know which firehouse he was assigned to. He just finished Probie School. When I got back home after the tournament, I had to work. I was sitting at the kitchen table, a couple of the brothers told me we were getting a new probie. We all waited at the table for this guy to walk through the door, when he came in, he was not a young looking kid. He had to be in his mid-thirties. He came in, and I started to joke around with him to see how he would take it. He told me his name, and I couldn't believe it. He was the guy that my friend told me about. The odds of that happening are over 500 to 1. We had this friend in common who I just met. It was like God directed him into my firehouse so we could help one another out. Later on, he would pay the ultimate sacrifice...

20

Never Let Your Guard Down

We had a job one night where the people who lived in the house were screaming, "My babies are in the house!" One of the brothers asked them where the baby might be. The women told us that they are hiding under a bed. The truckies ran in looking for the baby. All they came out with were two lifeless dogs and three puppies that were motionless. When the women seen the dogs and the puppies she said, "You found my babies!!" See the women was talking about her pets. What she did was put all the brothers who went back into the apartment in danger. There could have been a flashover that would have gotten someone either burnt really bad or killed. As for dogs, I am a dog lover but not at the risk of losing one of the brothers. When they laid the dogs on the grass near the sidewalk, I seen the mother dog was coughing and spit up and tried to wake up but was having a hard time getting to her feet. The puppies looked like they didn't make it. So I went over and picked one up and started to give it CPR by giving it breath through the mouth and snout and rubbing the stomach. One of the brothers came over and seen the puppy come back to life. He grabbed one and started mouth to mouth on another one and he spit up and started to breath on his own. My puppy, I laid down on the ground and the mother came over and laid next to them like a worried mother would. I picked up the last puppy and started CPR and that puppy started to move around. The other bigger dog we rubbed his stomach and started CPR for him but it was too late for the dog. It was a bitter sweet night we saved 4 and lost one, but the thought of possibly losing a brother over someone not using good judgment in telling firefighters that it was her dogs that she called her babies was scary. I know how I felt about my dogs and could give her a break-- but put the responsibility on us (firefighters) to ask.

(A routine run) .... It was a beautiful Sunday morning we get a run for an odor of gas. It was a building on Grand Concourse. As we got on the rig (fire truck), we responded 2nd due engine as we got up to the building. It was so nice out we all got on the back step figuring that it would be another 10-40 code 1 which means an odor of gas or gas leak. The first due truck and the chief went into the basement apartment to the area where the gas was reported and spoke to the super of the building. We were all on the back step of the firetruck. Some guys took off their turnout coat and we were trying to figure out what we were going to make for lunch, when all of a sudden we hear a blast and smoke starts flowing out of the manhole cover! Then we hear MAYDAY!! MAYDAY!! We all jumped up, and started over to the alleyway leading to the basement apartment. As we rounded the corner, the first due engine went down the alley and when we got down the alley the brothers were pulling out the chief, his driver (aid), the irons man and the lieutenant. They were covered in blood. The officer looked like he lost his eye. The others were bleeding from the face and head and the arm. They called an ambulance. We started to do first aid on the brothers that were bleeding badly from facial wounds. The officer didn't lose his eye, but he did have facial fractures. The others suffered broken bones in their face, shoulders and wrist. They had gone down to the electric panel and were shutting off the power to the building. When they shut off the power, the spark ignited the methane gas from the sewer. When the irons man shut the electric switch it lit up the gas and caused an explosion causing the 4-foot-high and 3-foot-wide steel panel to sheer off all the screws holding it together and hit all the brothers standing in front of it. Where they stood is basically what determined who got the worst injuries. The chief was hit in the face and shoulder. The officer from the truck had been hit in the face, others had broken bones in the hands and wrist and the truck officer had to get a metal plate put in his face. He would later come back to work as a firefighter again. When the electric

142

company got to the building, they explained things we had never heard of. It was whenever you have an odor of gas, never shut off the electric standing in front of the panel because the spark will cause an explosion. A very costly lesson that almost killed some of the brothers. God was watching over them that day. It also taught us to never let your guard down at any run or emergency....

21

My Safe Haven

When things were seeming to come together in the firehouse, my personal life was a 10-75 (working fire). I had my son and daughter living with my mother and my other two sons living in the Bronx. My plan all along was to have all of us to live in one house as a family but the boy's mother was against it and led me on to think that it was going to be that way. You see I was going back and forth between my kids upstate and my sons living in the Bronx. I would stay upstate a few days till I had to work then come down to the firehouse and work. Then I would stay with my sons in the Bronx. It was like being in a triangle. My life was going in circles. All I wanted was to have a family and settle down, but when I asked my sons mother to get married she said, "I have no intentions of raising your children." I was heartbroken because all my dreams were thrown out. I bought a house upstate and that's when things really hit a bad note. You see my family was grieving from the loss of my father and I was trying to keep all the kids together. I was trying to make things work, but I was being torn between spending time with my children and trying to fix a relationship that was not worth fixing. The firehouse was my only haven. When I was working, it seemed my problems were forgotten. I would sit at the kitchen all night talking to the brothers getting advice and laughing at crazy thoughts about finding a tropical island and moving there with the kids and live happily ever after. See the firehouse was a place where you could leave all your troubles at the door and if you brought them in, you might find someone to show you some sympathy. When guys had real problems, there was always someone to talk to, but if you came in with a girlfriend or "life's little bumps in the road problems'" you would be in for a ball busting experience. This would all come to an end a few years later when the unthinkable would happen which changed all the rules......

22

Back at E81

It was nice to be back home in E81 from where this story all started. You see the guys were young and hungry to fight fires and to learn. The officers in the house where a great mixture of experience. There were officers coming from busy companies throughout the city, but we had a few officers whose *elevator didn't go to the top floor* like one lieutenant in Engine 42. He had lived in Brooklyn, and there was a rumor about him that ended up being fact. He lived in a vacant building with his wife. He was white, and she was a black woman. He reminded me of the movie *Silence of the Lambs.* The guy who was the murderer and danced around the house dressed like women with his penis between his legs. *It puts the lotion on lol.* This officer would dye his hair a different color every couple of weeks, one-week orange, blond the next week, jet black, then for St. Patrick's Day he went green. One day I was getting off work and the brothers went out on a run. This officer was sitting at the kitchen table alone with no one else in the firehouse. We had a discussion about how much we loved the job, and he suggested that we should do it for free. I said Lieutenant, "Why do you think we should do it for nothing?" He said, "Are you kidding me? We eat well, they (city) give us water and heat and even give us cots to sleep in. Right then and there I realized he did live in a vacant building. So this must be like heaven to him. He then tells me about wanting to get rid of his wife!! I was like in shock! He was the type of guy that never smiled so I was like, "What were you thinking to do with her, divorce her?" He said, "No, I want to have her killed!" I laughed and waited for him to smile back, but he didn't. This wacko was serious! *I thought of the wildest thing I could think of and told him, "Llisten, If you want the spot (lieutenant job) why don't you ask one of the other lieutenants to bring your check home, and you wait till he gets inside and then you*

147

walk in and shoot your wife and the other lieutenant, then take off their clothes and say you caught them having an affair, and it was a crime of passion!" I said, *"Now you got rid of your wife, and you got an opening for a lieutenant's spot in the firehouse, and you killed two birds with one stone."* I laughed, and he looked at me with a weird smile and said, *"That's a great idea!"* Well, when I left the firehouse I called the officer and warned him to tell all the lieutenants in the house not to take a check to this wacko's house. A few years later he would die of Aids. But, besides being crazy, he was great at a fire; he was calm and cool, never panic or screamed.

A screamer was an officer that would be screaming from the moment you pulled up to the job until we put the fire out. To work with a screamer was terrible because if you had a probie, you didn't want the kid to get scared. The more you panic, the more air you use, and you would be useless or take a feed (overcome with smoke). We had this one lieutenant I worked with. The man was a screamer at a fire and was about 5'5". We used to say that he had a Napoleon complex. (A short person who is a boss of men and feels as though he has to push his power around to make up for his lack of height). This lieutenant came from a good firehouse that had a reputation of being great at fires. This guy went to the house stayed there for a cup of coffee and then went to become a Battalion Aid so that he could study to take the lieutenant's test. When he got on the officers list, he went back to the busy house and got promoted out of there. Now he can tell everyone that he worked in a busy house, but we all know the truth now. LOL! He was the one officer that no one wanted to work with. He would make a night tour drag even if you were running all night. His biggest thing was he had to sit at the head of the table when we had chow. He would get at the table early just to sit there. He also said he didn't like tuna fish and "chicken on the bone", and he wanted a fresh pot of coffee made when he comes into work and after chow. One time he had the nerve after dinner to grab the coffee pot and started shaking it for one of the brothers to get up and make him coffee! The brother, a senior man

149

with more time then Lt. Napoleon turned around and said, "Lieutenant, you take the filter, and you put it in the coffee holder, and then you take those silver packets that hold the coffee grinds and then hit that button, and it makes a fresh pot of coffee." He was pissed. He was speechless. He stormed up to the office. He later called the probies into the office and told them it was their job to make sure he has coffee. So a couple of days later, I am working, and the probies are scrambling around worrying about getting the coffee ready for Lt Napoleon. They made a fresh pot and put it in a large coffee dispenser that held about 12 cups. I told them, "You really did this for this guy!" They told me about the meeting he had after the coffee caper. I told them not to buckle under the pressure of that guy. They went up front to relieve the house watchmen. I went over to the 12 cup dispenser and dumped the whole thing. O yea!! I took the dispenser and put dishwashing liquid in it and had foam flowing out the top into the sink. When Lieutenant Napoleon came in he had a fit. He called the probies into the kitchen and started screaming at them. I walked into the kitchen and said,

"Wait that was a fresh pot of coffee? I didn't know that." I was cleaning it out for your boss." The brother looked at me and smiled. He said, "See lieutenant we had it made." I said, "I am sorry boss!" He said to me, "Don't call me boss! You call me Lieutenant!!" He stomped up the stairs. I told the probies to call him Lieutenant Dick!! We all laughed and couldn't believe how much of an asshole he was. When we got the meal that night... you got that right, "chicken on the bone!!" He had to order pizza and still have to pay for the meal. You cannot act like that and think your life in the firehouse is going to go smoothly -the brothers always stick together.

23

God Works in Mysterious Ways-The Mosaic

As I sit on this mountain reflecting back on my
return to Engine 81, I can't help but have my
thoughts wander to the beautiful Mosaic that
hangs in the Firehouse. The story of the Mosaic
is an important part of my journey and key to
the blinders that have come off and have
helped me spiritually on my journey. It is a bit
of a long story, but here we go... A good friend
of mine owned a septic company out in
Missouri and had done work for me out there. I
never met his wife but I talked to her a lot
during the time the work was getting done. Her
name was Rusty. I had sold my house out there
and was going there to pick up things and bring
them back to New York. During September 11,
2001 Rusty called me to make sure I was alright.

She would check in with me a couple times a week. I went out to pick up my things in Missouri in 2003, two years or so after 9-11. As I loaded my truck, I thought it would be nice to stop and see Jerry and Rusty and tell them thanks for their help. I stopped by the office and seen this woman behind the counter, and she said, "You must be Chris Edwards. My name is Rusty." She came around the counter and gave me a hug. She said that she was praying for me and others down at the Trade Center, and she had a gift that she was holding to give to me so I could take it to the firehouse and hang it up in my firehouse for all the firefighters who died on 9-11. She told me she went to a high school in Missouri and bought it from an auction being held at the school. I could not thank her enough, a lot of tears and hugs and I told her that I was going to bring it to my firehouse and hang it up alongside the brothers' pictures that died on the job and on 9/11. On the way home, my son Travis and I drove a U-Haul back to NY. I called my brother Steve who lives out in Missouri to tell him the story about the mosaic. My brother asked me what it looked like, and I explained it to him that she went and bought it from an auction at some high school. My brother said to tell my sister-in-law (Sue) the story. Sue asked me what it looked like, and I told her it was like tiles glued together to make the American Flag. She asked me what the woman's name was, and I told her Rusty and her husband's name is Jerry. Now my brother lives about four hours away from Rusty and Jerry. Sue told me that it was her high school that sold the mosaic to a woman and her husband, and they had asked her what she was going to do with it. She told her she was going to give it to an NYC Firefighter that she knew to put in his firehouse. You see that woman that Sue spoke to was Rusty! They never met before but Rusty just so happen to stop by this school out of the blue to see what was for sale and bought the mosaic from my sister-in-law! God really works in ways we cannot explain. We must ride the wave of life and have faith in God, and all things will work out... that's how it works!! Now this mosaic hangs in the firehouse surrounded by firefighters who have died from the house.

24

My Second Job!

My side job takes off, and while getting back to E81 was a great start, the brothers were hearing about the acting jobs that were coming in for me. I had a great partner who would work around my schedule. I didn't want the fire department to become my second job. If the casting agent called for an audition and I didn't make it then I would probably would not have gotten a callback. Fortunately, there was always someone in the firehouse that would step up (work the tour). The biggest thing was they wanted to see me on the TV or the big screen. You see the brother who got me involved said that if I joined the actors union I would be working all the time, and he was right. I started playing firefighters on movies and then I was casted to portray cops in movies. When I needed a cop uniform, all the brothers that transferred from the NYPD had their old uniforms and wanted me to wear it. One of the brothers gave me his hat; another gave me his holster and another gave me his uniform. By the time I was done I had a full cop uniform; plus, I already had the firefighter's uniform. None of them wanted money they just said make my uniforms famous. I started getting calls to do background work as police officers. We would shoot a TV show, and the brothers would be all sitting around the kitchen table waiting for the show to air. They were all great when the part came on, they would get up and go crazy...*hey, that's my hat, Hey that's my shirt and those are my pants.* They had a lot of fun with it. The career was "acting career" full steam ahead! There were other firefighters in the acting business, and they weren't doing as well as I was and I would hear some rumors about these brothers that would say they were better actors than me. They were the ones who made acting their first job. I didn't want to leave the fire department, but they would have. Some people would have called me crazy, but my heart was all about fighting fires and being the best firefighter I could be. Then the acting job became bigger, and I got lines in movies and TV shows, to the point where I would need a week off. I got to shoot the movie *Extreme Measures.* I worked with Hugh Grant. I played the arresting officer with lines and everything. The brothers went crazy when they saw it in the movies. I started working on the Conan O'Brien show as the regular cop and then the TV show, "The Nanny". Other shows started calling me for more cop roles. I started working on soap operas, playing cops and detectives and the comedy series *John Leguizamo Show* as a firefighter. I also worked with Howard Stern in *Private Parts* as a cop that escorts him out of Bryant Square Park. I worked with Mark Wahlberg, James Caan and Faye Dunaway in the movie *The Yards*. I worked with Wesley Snipes, Andy Garcia, Woody Harrelson among others the list was endless. I even had a hand modeling job for Panasonic Drills. I was working around the clock. My outside life was a mess. I was supporting my children with the money and living on the extra money I had left over which was a couple hundred dollars a week. It was tough, but I knew God had a hand in this because I would pray to some day to be able to take care of my family and everything just fell into place. I would talk to my father at his grave site and even when I was alone or going in for an audition, I would then land the job. See my father was a cop, and I got cop jobs. I knew he never left my side. Even when I needed him the most, as I would see in the future, my father was always around me!

25

Death Does Not Discriminate

Death doesn't discriminate. Transferring to Engine 81, north of Engine 42 you would think the violence would not follow. Comparing the neighborhoods, Engine 42 was more in the streets. It was off a major highway, and the area had more working people coming and going to work every morning. The difference was that there were more people going to work and heading to the train. Figuring this, you would think that crime in this area was lower, but I would find out that it would not matter. See we got an EMS run about an apartment door open and a possibly abandoned baby left in the bedroom by herself. We head to the address, and when we get there, the door was open to the apartment, so we call out for someone, and we don't get an answer. So the captain says to go search the rooms. We go through the kitchen and then the living room and then the bathroom and everything is clear. When we get to the bedroom, the door was open just a crack to be able to see in. As we got closer to the room, you could hear cartoons on the TV. The room was a mess as we opened the door. There were clothes all over the floor and on the bed was a three-year-old little girl sitting there eating potato chips. We asked her where her mommy or daddy was, and she pointed to the floor on the other side of the bed. I walked around and saw a women face down and with nothing on from the waist down. I told the captain, and I went over and asked her if she was OK and there was no response, so I went to check her pulse. I see that she had post-mortem hypostasis (pooling of the blood on the body). I told the captain that she was dead. The captain called for the police. The EMTs got there as I was looking for her pulse on her carotid artery. I see something wrapped around her neck like someone had strangled her. The captain looked and said don't touch the body and let's back out of the room to preserve a possible crime scene. NYPD showed up and said they might need to speak to us later to figure out what happened. We went back to quarters, and the captain got us all together and went over everything we saw and touched. Later that day the NYPD called up and said they needed to speak to all the brothers that were in the room. We all got together, and they questioned us on what we touched, seen, and what condition and position the body was in because they were doing a crime scene investigation. Later that week they called us back and said that the women died of a heart attack, and they were ruling it a natural death. That little girl sat in the room with her mother's partially nude body for over 8 hours. Thank God that little girl had no clue what happened to her mother. She was sent to live with an aunt. See this is just how it went on the job. I just couldn't get away from death.

A week later we had another EMS run. The dispatcher said that the 911 caller stated that his father was laying on the floor in the living room naked for about a week. This was at the

161

housing projects (low and moderate-income residents). We had the same crew working for the last EMS run. This call was a lot crazier!! We get to the apartment door, and the door is cracked open. We knock, and no one answers. "Fire Dept!!" No answer, so we open the door a little more and say, "Fire Dept!!" We look around, and the whole room was covered with trash and garbage on the floor, roaches running on the walls and food left on the stove with green mold growing on it. Now we hear someone in the back bedroom say, "He's on the floor in the living room!!" The captain asked, "Who are you?" The voice in the room said, "I am his son, and my father has been lying on the floor for a week and he is not moving." We could smell something rotten but didn't know if it was the garbage or something else. As we walked into the living room, you could see the naked body of a man face down in the trash. I went over to the body and when I went to check the pulse, I seen maggots crawling out of the ears and nose. The captain told me not to touch the body. We backed out of the room and the captain called out to the son in the back bedroom, who never came out to speak to us.

The EMTs are going to work on your father. The son never responded. The NYPD showed up, and we took up (back to quarters) when we got back everyone cleaned out their boots and bunker gear. We were so worried about the roaches in the apartment. A couple of days later one of the brothers reads a story in the paper about a son who confessed to murdering his father for drug money and then left his nude body for a week in their apartment. We were all like that was the old man we saw! Who would have known if the son happened to have a weapon on him when we walked in? God was with us. That's why I would never let my guard down on any calls.

Another run we had during my time with Engine 81 was a call to something on the railroad tracks above the Bronx/ Manhattan Bridge. As we responded, we could see people looking over the side. Cars pulling over to see what it was. Some of them were holding young children ages 6 to 8 years old pointing to this thing on the tracks. We cleared some of the cars off the bridge. We looked over and could see a bike all mangled up. Next to the bike it looked like a pair of pants. When you looked around you could make out a body of someone. We walked down to the tracks, and the cops were keeping traffic moving. We see that it was a man that had been hit by the metro north train. His body was torn to pieces. The bike was about 50 yards from the body. When we looked under the bridge, we could see where he had been hit. There was blood spatter about 10 feet high on the bridge wall. I thought how sick these people were for picking little children up and pointing out the body of this poor soul. It seems that death to some people was exciting, but then again nobody turns their head away from an accident. As for me, I had seen it all and found no pleasure or excitement from a dead body. I would always say a prayer for the dead. It would stay with me for the rest of my life, but it's like a learning experience. Because of what I learned with dealing with death on the job, I thought I had seen it all until September 11, 2001. That was beyond anything I could ever imagine. It will haunt me forever!!

We get a run at about 12:30 am on a Friday night for a woman on the sidewalk laying down. This was near the reservoir, a decent area in our district. A predominantly Spanish neighborhood. We get to the scene, and there is a young white woman laying on the sidewalk. Standing next to her was a guy who said he was her boyfriend. We asked him what had happened to her, and he said she had collapsed as they were walking home. When we checked for her pulse, her face had turned blue, and she was breathing very shallow. We looked around the area and found a needle on the ground not too far away from her. We asked the boyfriend if it was hers. He told us no. We looked at him and said, *"You have to tell us the truth if you want to save your girlfriend."* He still denied it, but we looked and seen a needle mark on her arm and told him... *she is not going to make it if you don't tell us the truth.* At that point, EMS arrived, and we gave them the information and said that it looks like she OD on heroin. The EMS workers gave her a shot of Narcan, and the girl came out of it. We looked at the boyfriend, a white male about 20 years old, and told him that he shouldn't be in that neighborhood. His girlfriend was a beautiful young woman about 18 years old. He said that it was the first time that they tried heroin and that they would never do it again. We went back to the firehouse and talked about those two young kids coming down to the Bronx and buying heroin. A couple of weeks later on a cold December night, we get an EMS run at about 4 am on a Sunday morning to an area near a mechanic's garage near a set of stairs leading up to a wealthy part of the Bronx. There on the steps were two people wrapped in a blanket. When we got next to them, we were heartbroken to see that it was that young couple again. This time, they had wrapped themselves in a blanket when we took the blanket off they were in their underwear. The guy had his arm wrapped around his girlfriend. She was in a bra and panties. We checked her pulse, and she had none. EMS pulled up and gave her a shot of Narcan, and she was unresponsive. She was pronounced dead at the scene. The boyfriend was crying as they took his girlfriend away. I said a prayer for that young girl weeks before and I guess it was not answered. Now you have a wasted life. I could never understand the power of a drug that people could die from. All during my career at Engine 81, I saw more heroin abuse in the good neighborhoods. The vicious cycle of drugs holds no boundaries!

26

Different Neighborhood, Same Results

Like in E42 I would always make it a habit to get to know people in and around the firehouse. The location of the firehouse was a spot where people are going and coming to work had to cross to make it to the train or the shops on Broadway in the Bronx. I would try and greet people coming and going to work whenever I could like I did at E42. Meet the people, get to know them, put a face on the neighborhood you work in. I knew the good people, and I knew the trouble makers of the neighborhood, and I knew who the drug addicts were. See you can tell after working in bad neighborhoods who are trying to rip you off and those who are just down on their luck.

There was a woman who I spoke to a couple of times. Her name was Lovette. You could see that she was a drug abuser. She would always come by the firehouse and knock on the door and ask for money. So one day I answered the door and told her, "I will not give you money, but I will buy you food." She said she was not hungry, and I asked her what she was going to do if I gave her money. She said, "Chris I am not going to lie to you, I am going to buy drugs." I told her, "I will feed you, but I will never give you money because you are killing yourself!" She was not happy, and as she walked away, I told her I was only doing it for her own good. She turned and smiled and said, "You really do care about me." I told her Yes!! Then she walked away. About a couple days later it was snowing, and I see her walking up the block with a laundry cart. Inside the cart was a little girl about two years old with PJ's on and no coat and it was snowing! She comes up to cross the street, and I run out of firehouse door and ask her where the babies coat is? She tells me she was in a rush to go to the store. See this little girl was her daughter! Lovette couldn't care for herself, how in the hell is she going to take care of this baby? I told her to take the baby home and get her a jacket. She looked at me and said ok and turned around and came back 10 minutes later with the baby's coat on. See she didn't understand that I could care for her. Well, what kind of love was her daughter getting? I told her I would say a prayer for her and her daughter. She was surprised that I believed in God. I told her I pray for my family and friends. She was so addicted to drugs she was numb. There were other times where she would come by and say she was hungry, so we would walk down the street and put an order in the Chinese restaurant, and the workers would stare at me because they knew her act. I would ask her what she wanted to eat. She would order "fried chicken wings and pork fried rice combo and a Hi-C." I would pay the bill then tell the worker, "Whatever you do, don't let her cancel the order and take the money." I used to tell Lovette that when she would get her life straightened out, I want her to pull up in front of the firehouse in a stretch limo and get out all dressed up and say, "Chris I am taking you to dinner." I knew it would never happen, but it gave her a positive image to live with to try and help her beat the habit. I didn't believe it, but I wanted her to.

I pretty much had it worked out with the Chinese restaurant and a Bodega (Spanish grocery store) when I would buy food for some of the people. They were always the same cast of characters, some needed and others tried to con me. During this time, I met so many great people who lived in the neighborhood, and I became really good friends with a lot of them. Like a gentleman by the name Barney. He was an old Irishman right off the boat with the Irish brogue. He and I would talk on the days I was working. We got to know one another so well that we would do breakfast at the diner. He would want to pay, but I never let him. He was a great man. He told me his wife was in a nursing home because of Alzheimer's disease. He felt as though he could no longer care for her because he also suffered from a heart failure. But every day he would walk about two miles to see her and eat lunch and dinner with her. Barney and I would talk for hours when I wasn't working. If I was getting off of work in the morning, I would drive him up to the nursing home. He had one son, but he had a life of his own. I found out one Thanksgiving that he was by himself, and I invited him into the firehouse for dinner. He had a great time, and other holidays that I wasn't working, I would have the brothers make a plate for him and deliver it to his apartment.

Across the street from the firehouse there were a lot of old Irish families. They were still holding strong in changing times. There were a lot of Latin families moving around the area. Some good and others bad, but for the most part, the people in the building were great people. Another friend I made was a man named John. He looked like Errol Flynn. He told me he was in acting and had done some plays in the city. He would walk his German Shepherd in the empty lot near the firehouse. He would tell me stories of when he was young and his girlfriends. He was never married and one time I set him up with another woman from Monroe Avenue. They went out on a date that really didn't go too well. I never heard the end of it from the two of them. He said all she does is talk about herself, and she would tell me all he does is talk about himself. Perfect match. Lol!! There were other real nice people with unbelievable stories of a lifetime of great memories. The guys in the firehouse were a little more understanding on befriending people in the neighborhood because once I introduced them they realized that they were good people. Knowing the area and the people living around the firehouse is very important. See a lot of the brothers like to keep the door shut and come and go to work without getting to meet people. This was important because they are the eyes around the House when it matters the most, at night and when you go out on runs, your cars are parked on the street. One day I had the doors open, and I was on house watch when I see this old man walk on the other side of the Rig (truck). I go over to the man, and I ask him if he would like a tour of the truck. He says, "No I am meeting my wife at church." I felt as if the man was suffering from Alzheimer's disease. I knew something was not right, so I say, "Do you know where you are right now?" He says, "Yes I am at the church." I asked him his name, and he said it was Louie. I told him to sit down, and I will call his wife, but he couldn't remember his phone number. I asked him if I could look in his wallet and maybe find it. One of the other brothers were with me when I looked and couldn't find a number, but I see on his wrist he had a medical bracelet on that said "Safe Return." It was an 800 number and it ID'd him as an Alzheimer's patient. I called the number, and ID'd myself to the operator and told her that Louie had walked into the firehouse and that he was safe. They told me to keep him there and that they were calling his family. A few minutes later his wife called crying saying that he walked out the door when she was doing laundry and couldn't find him. I told her the address, and she came down to pick him up and was so grateful. During that time, Louie and I talked and became friends. A couple of months later I was working out in the firehouse when I got off work, and I look out the window and who do I see but Louie walking across the street up the hill to a bad section of the neighborhood. I called out his name, and he stopped and looked around till he seen me. I told him to wait, and I will give him a ride. I get him into the firehouse and ask him where he was going to. He said, "I am going to a party." I took him into the firehouse, and we sat down and talked. I called the "Safe Return" number again and I ID'd myself again and said, "Does this always happen, that someone calls twice on the same person?" His family showed up and were very thankful again and called me. Louie's guardian angel. I thought to myself, God put me there for a reason. Who would have known what might have happened if I wasn't there? About six months later I received a letter at the firehouse from the "Safe Return" program for Alzheimer's patients. They wanted to give me an award for the safe return of Louie at One Police Plaza. I went with my family and was given the award by the Police Commissioner Bernard Kerik. I was the First New York City Firefighter to receive the Safe Return Award. See if you don't get involved you cannot help out. That's why I always told the probies, get to know the people in the neighborhood!

27

Some Doors Close... Other Doors Open

Things at the firehouse were going well. We were getting jobs every tour. You have to get it while it's hot I would say. See fires come in spurts, you would be very busy, and then you could be on a cool spell. A lot had to do with the weather, and some had to do with holidays, like July 4th and full moons. It sounds crazy, but it was true. The colder the weather, the more people would use anything to stay warm. You see we were hot and at any time, it could go cold real fast. It's like catching the right groups. The groups that were hot would call the slower group the black cloud. While things were good at the firehouse, my personal life was a 10-75 -- all hands fire, even at some points it went to a 5 alarm fire!! I had my third son born on April 18,

1995. This date would later play a big part in both of our lives. As I was trying to get a family started with someone who wasn't right for me, I struggled between trying to make everybody happy and in the end making nobody happy. My escape was the firehouse. It was Super Bowl Sunday back in 1999. It was a slow day. We had a couple of small fires a few days before. Usually on Sunday's, the day seemed to be slow. This Sunday was going to be different. It was going to be one of the worst days of my career. It was in the afternoon when someone comes running to the firehouse saying there was smoke pouring out three windows on the first floor of an H-type apartment building. When you get a verbal in the daytime, you know it's for real. It's just a matter of finding out how big it would be. So we turn out the engine and the truck and drive down the block, seeing the smoke coming out of three windows on the first-floor apartment. Now being aggressive, I jump off the rig and grab the knob and a length of hose and jumped off the back step. Never realizing that there was a loose cobble stone. When I hit the ground my knee buckled and I hear a pop! The pain was intense.

177

One of the brothers seen me down and went to grab the knob away from me, I jumped up and said, "Hell no!!" And stretched the line into the apartment. We had a solid three rooms of fire. The whole time I wasn't even thinking about my knee. We knocked it down (got it under control) it took about 10 minutes. All along feeling a burning inside my knee. I knew I would be in trouble. When I got in the street and the adrenaline started to lose its painless effect. I rolled down my bunker gear and seen a knee that was the size of a grapefruit. One of the brothers went over to the officer and said I took a bad fall. He came over and asked how I felt. I said, "I need to get an MRI on it." Feeling the pain, I knew right away. They took me to Columbia Presbyterian in Manhattan. They brought me into the emergency room and took X-rays. Finding there were chipped bones of the fibular, they said I had to follow up with an orthopedic doctor when I get back home. I needed a ride back to the Bronx to get to the firehouse. I called the FDNY van to pick me up and the brother told me he was in Staten Island, and he could not make it for an hour or so. He said he was watching the Super Bowl and

178

couldn't make it down to get me. Remember that 1%? There he is. You never leave a brother who was in the hospital to get a ride back to the firehouse because, in order for me to get back up to the Bronx, I had to hit the subway. When I got up to the firehouse just in time to watch the Broncos crush the Falcons. This just added insult to injury. I just miss hitting the pool for $500. This was just the start of my bad luck and the long road back to recovery. See the following day I had to go to the FDNY medical office. Nobody wants to go to the medical office. The doctors do whatever they can to make things difficult on you, that you want to heal right away. My Injuries didn't show up on the X-rays, so I had to make an appointment with an orthopedic doctor. He sent me in for an MRI on the knee. I went home and came back a couple of days later. He called me into his office and sat me down and told me that there was no way I was going to be able to work with a knee like this. You have a partial tear of your anterior cruciate ligament ... also known as the ACL. It is the ligament that gives your knee stability. It keeps it from buckling. He also said that I had damage to the meniscus. It is the cartilage disk that's found in the knee. I tore it, and he told me I had bone chips from the fibula. He asked me if I was ready to retire. I was shocked! I said, "Doc, I want to work. I love the job. I couldn't see myself without the fire department in my life. I had found the greatest job in the world, why would I want to leave it!" He told me that he would have to go in and do orthopedic surgery and that it would take about three months to get back to the firehouse. I was all geared up to have this and get back to work, but the doctor told me before the operation that my knee was so bad that he felt that it will give out and have to be replaced in the future. I didn't want to hear that. I figured I could keep working and do about 30 years, but I was only fooling myself. I went back to the FD medical office and seen this old doctor who had been there for years. He said that he wanted me to start physical therapy in about two weeks. I started going, and I was on a mission to get back to the firehouse. After about two months of physical therapy, I felt better but I was still sore. I go back to the fire department doctor, and he said, "I am going to put you on light duty for a couple of months." I thought to myself, "If

I can do light duty, I can do full duty." That was a mistake I will regret to this day. I told the doctor I want to go full duty. He said, "You were ready to go back to the firehouse?" I told him yes. He told me he was going to bring in two other doctors, and they would make a decision to see if I can go back. They had me crawl on the floor. I had to fight back the pain; then they told me to do a duck walk. It is what we do when we are fighting a fire stay low and walk on your heel and toes. I wanted to scream, but I held back the screams and the tears just to get by the three doctors. They all agreed that I could go back to full duty. Yes!! Back to the brothers and the safe haven from my personal life.

When I got back to the firehouse, the brothers started joking about never coming back. They were surprised to see me after 2 1/2 months from surgery. I explained to them that I was still hurting, but I didn't want to go on light duty. The brothers would help me out if we got a job and others would give me a break not letting me work going up and down the stairs. I was in pain, but I would not let anyone see it. Then the captain called me into the office and told me he thinks it would be a great idea for me and my career if I go to the Chauffeur School and drive the engine. He felt being I was a senior man, and I knew the neighborhood and the area that it would extend my career, but I was young and dumb. See I felt if you are not on the back step you were not a firefighter. I thought I had a lot of firefighting left in me than to be standing at the rig watching from the outside. I was dead wrong, and I would learn the hard way. Always listen to the captain's orders! He was right because after six months of full duty and pushing the knee and not taking it easy on my body, the knee was about ready to give way. See we had a job at a laundry mat. It was the lint tray on top of the dryers that caught fire. A real shitty job, because of the smoke and we had to climb onto and squeeze in between the wall and the dryer. As I was climbing the ladder, my knee gave way, and I almost fell and hit the captain behind me. He saw the knee buckle and said, "What the hell happened?" I told him my foot slipped off the ladder. He said, "Bullshit, I seen that knee buckle! You are going to get that knee checked before you hurt yourself or one of the brothers." I knew he was right, but I knew it was the end of my fire department career, but I always had hope that it would all work out, but, I was in for a rough road ahead!

28

Hope and a Dream

I knew when the captain called me out over the slip on the ladder that the possible road I would have to take to get back was going to be tough, so I went to the hospital that night and was told to see the fire department orthopedic doctor. I went down the next day, and I figured I would get the older doctor who I got to put me back to work early from the first operation, but I was called into the office, and I met a new doctor who just started working for the fire department. It always seems like when you see a doctor who has been with the fire department for a long time; they want to throw you back to work or make you stay on light duty and miserable. I told the doctor about my prior operations and what the doctor told me about the results of the MRI from eight months ago. She was so understanding that she asked me what I wanted to do. I explained to her that the job was my life; I didn't want to leave. I want to finish my career on my terms not to have it cut short by an injury. I had asked her what she thought my chances of making it back were. She said she would do whatever I needed her to do to keep me on the job. I knew right away that I was in good hands. Someone who really felt the way I did and didn't treat me like a piece of meat. She gave me authorization for a trip to my orthopedic doctor who had done the first operation. I got an appointment two days later because my doctor knew what he might have to do. Well during the time in between, I reflected on my path up to that point. I realized that it was going to be tough. Maybe one major operation and I could be back within a year. Only God knew what I was in store for. I went to the doctor, and he wasn't surprised to see me. He said, "Chris I knew it would be soon because your knee was shot a year ago." He asked me if I was ready to retire. I looked at him and said, "Doctor I don't know anything else but to be a firefighter." We discussed what my chances were and what the operation would pertain to. He said he had an operation that could get me back in a year. I asked him what would I have to go through to get back, and he said you know the fire department will not take you back with a knee replacement. I told him I want to go back no matter what I have to do, so we weighed out my options. He said there was an operation he could do that would get me back to work in six to eight months. The knee would be like new after it healed. It was called the *Worker Knee Replacement*. The medical term was Osteotomy ("bone cutting") which is a procedure where a surgeon removes a wedge of bone near a damaged joint. This shifts weight from an area where there is damaged cartilage to an area where there is healthier cartilage. It all had to do with bone work and reconstruction of the knee without plates and screws after it heals. Perfect! I told the doctor that if it can get me back to work within a year, I was all for it. Later that week I went back to see the fire department doctor, and she asked if I was willing to go through this to come back? I told her if I can make it back in a year, I would be willing to do it. She had more of a level headed

186

approach. She told me to ask my doctor three questions. 1) How many of these osteotomies has he done in his career? 2) How many has he done in a year? 3) What's the percentages rate of success? I was really glad to hear her say that because then I knew that she was willing to help me get back. I was so excited to have hope to get back that I called my doctor on the way home. He got on the phone, and I asked him the three questions. He said one osteotomy a year and 20 in his career and a 75% rate of success. I called the fire department doctor the next morning, and she asked me what I thought of my doctor's answer of 75% success rate. I told her that if I could get back to the firehouse with a 75% chance, I want to take it because my other chances were a lot less than that. Well, I told my doctor that I was willing to take his 75% and go with it. I called the next day, and we made the appointment for September 27, 2000. The beginning of what I knew would be a tough, but this fresh start was just going to get a lot tougher than any of us could imagine...

29

The Emotional Roller Coaster Begins...

I get my appointment for the operation and its full speed ahead. Not knowing what was in store for me a couple of days before the operation, I went to the firehouse to tell the captain my plans and he sat me down at the kitchen table and we talked about what the future would hold when I healed and came back full duty. Some of the other brothers came in and sat down to listen to what I thought was going to be a routine surgery. The brothers put it up on the board about me being in the hospital and told me to keep them informed on the room number. I was thinking there might be a crazy thing that they would deliver to me. I pity the poor nurses that would be subjected to some of their odd humor, but that was just the beginning. One of the senior men took me aside and told me there are guys on the job that would like the opportunity to be able to retire. I told him it is the last thing on my mind. I want to stay. He told me he knew I would be the guy they would have to carry out on a stretcher to leave this job. He shook my hand and wished me well. A couple of days later who could predict that it would be that way? My family couldn't understand why I would go through this type of complicated operation, but nobody really understands unless you are a firefighter. You see we know that the job is a calling, one that you cannot explain to civilians.

The day of the operation I went to church and said a prayer. I asked God to have everything go well and then I left it in his hands. I get to the hospital and sign all the papers just in case I would kick the bucket. They wheeled me into the operating room, and as I laid there, I looked over to my right and on a table were tools to be used for the operation. I thought it was a maintenance man's tool bucket. I saw a stainless steel sledgehammer, a hand saw, a screw gun and stainless steel chisels. I asked the nurse if that was all for me? She smiled and said yes as the anesthesiologist put the knock-out juice into my IV. When I came to, it was about three hours later. I asked the nurse how the operation went, and she said well. I was sick from the anesthesia when the doctor came in to see me and told me he would keep me overnight. Thank God because if I had gone home I just might have lost my leg. They put me into a room after I felt a little better. The nurse came in and said you have to urinate before midnight. She also came in with a machine that extended the knee back and forth to keep it from freezing up. The pain was unbelievable, and that was with medication. Now I was going to have my leg bending back and forth all night. I could see the bandage had gone from my hip all the way to my foot. There was a large spot of blood that ran the length of the leg. All night long I was praying to go to the bathroom so I could leave in the morning. I drank water all night and nothing! The nurse came in every hour asking if I went yet. I said no. Well, you have to go in order to be released. I told her to give me some time. The nurse said if you don't go we have to put a Foley catheter. I think to myself, I will be damned if I let a nurse put that in me. I even got up and disconnected the machine that kept pulling my knee back and forth in order to get up and put my hand under warm water... standing in pain. Nothing! Finally, on the change of shifts a nurse came in and said I have to get the catheter!! Damn, I just laid there thinking if this is what I have to go through to get back to the firehouse, then so be it. The nurse came in, and she pushed the tube in my penis and I filled up a bag and a half of urine. They left it in all night, and I figured I would be going home in the morning, but I didn't think I could make it with the pain. It was intense. The doctor did his morning rounds and asked me how I was feeling. I told him about the night, the machine and the pain, the urine and getting sick from the anesthesia. I asked him about the sledgehammer and chisels and if he used them on me. He said the operation was very difficult because he had to break the leg. Then he had to do a lot of bone work cutting, sawing and chiseling the bone to the right angel. He had to put a bone graft in between the two bones so it would grow and reconstruct the knee. He also told me about a high chance of infection because of the bone work. Wow, just think I could have retired. The thought was never in my mind. I want to make it back to the greatest job in the world. Well, the doctor cuts off the bandages, and a foul smell came from the operation sight. It smelled like rotten meat. He looked at the staples and seen swelling. He told me that I was going to have to stay another night because of the swelling and the smell. He was concerned because he felt there was an infection. Great another night in the hospital!

The night was another painful night. A catheter in and a machine moving my leg back and forth. The nurse would hook me up, and when she left, I would wiggle the plug till it fell out of the socket. The doctor also put me on powerful IV antibiotics, hoping that it would get clear up the infection or at least prevent it. When the doctor did his rounds the next day, he looked at the wound and told me he had to go back in and clean it out because there was an infection. He would have to go in and clean it out and keep me in the hospital for a couple of days more. So the nurses prepared me for my second operation in two days. Well for an operation that was supposed to be same day, I ended up being in there 17 days! The infection had healed up, and I was ready to take my first steps to get back to the firehouse. During that time in the hospital, the brothers called and sent flowers and brought food and one brother sneaked in a *Playboy* magazine with a *Field and Stream* cover. They had me laughing the whole time, even with the physical pain. You see it's the Brotherhood that follows you inside and outside of the firehouse!

30

Disappointment, Pain, and Heartache but Still Determined

For the next three weeks, I had to walk with crutches. The pain level was at seven on a good day and ten on all the others. You see I was walking on a broken leg which was being held together by a metal bracket with four screws. I had an appointment with the fire department doctor who was upset with all that I had gone through with the infection. She was a so helpful and supportive on anything I needed to do to get back on the job. My appointment with my doctor was a couple of days away. I had an apartment in the Bronx. The problem was that it was a walk up, so for the time being I was staying at my aunt's house upstate, in her finished basement. She was like a mother to me and helped me get back on my feet. My doctor's office was in the town of Warwick, NY, which is also upstate that made living with my aunt also convenient.

There is a church in the Bronx called Saint Lucy's with a grotto in front with a spring of fresh water running through it. These waters are known to be holy. People come from all over to fill bottles of holy water. Some worshipers put water on their face and wash their hands, and others pour it over their heads like a Baptism; others would put it on their cars to bless it and protect it, but when they drive away I could tell they needed more than God's blessing to protect them. Well, I would go to St Lucy's a couple of times a week to sit there and pray and take some holy water and wash it down the leg, all along keeping my eye on my goal of getting back to the brothers and the greatest job in the world. Well, the day came that I had my doctor appointment and the doctor said to me, "I cannot believe you are back to see me after all you have been through." I told him that he gave me my chances and the warning of infection and that I didn't blame him for it. I told him it's in God's hands now. He sent me for X-rays in the office. Afterward, I went back to talk to him about the X-rays. He read them and said you are really going to hate me. It seems the bone graft was eaten by the infection. This is why you have so much pain. You have been walking on a broken leg for the last three weeks. The only thing holding it together is the metal plates and screws. I asked him what we do next. He looked at me and said, "I have to go back in and remove all the hardware and force the two bones together to stimulate bone growth." I told him whatever we have to do to get back to the firehouse I am willing to do it. He looked at me and said, "I know firefighters love their job, but I have never seen anybody so determined to get back to work as you." I told him that words cannot describe the love I have for the job, the brothers and the ability to help people. He shook his head, and a smile came to his face and he said, "Are you ready for the next step?" I shook my head and told him, "Let's do it!" He told me that when he takes the plates and screws out, I would have to walk with a cane and put full weight on it. I thought...great more pain. I went to the FD doctor and told her what was going on, and she asked me, "Chris do you really want to go through with this?" I told her yes. In the weeks that followed, I went into the hospital, and the doctor took the screws and plates out in October 2000, and I started the next phase of my painful comeback. I never gave up on my faith and that God would make all this craziness work. I figured that this was just another test.

 During the next months of walking in pain, we lost seven firefighters and one EMT officer all from November 2000 to August 2001. Every one of those deaths made my fight to get back to the greatest job in the world a mission!! During this time, I started to do light duty at the Rock (Randall's Island) the FDNY training center, for about a month. Still feeling pain in both my leg and my heart for the loss of these brothers who lost their lives fighting fires, I went back to my doctor with more X-rays of the knee, and he told me that there was no bone growth. He said the only thing left to do was to do the Osteotomy all over again. I was devastated, but still had a lot of hope and determination and fight to get back. I went back with the message from my doctor and spoke to the FD doctor and sat down and explained the next step and started crying. She got up and closed the door, and we cried together. She was so upset that it all came out after three operations two and half weeks in the hospital and still no positive results. She looked at me and said, "Are you sure you want this? I told her yes. So she suggested another opinion...down to Manhattan I went. I went to a well-known doctor who refused to operate because I had been opened before. Still my search for a solutions and answers had begun...never giving up on God, but questioning my faith a lot more. Questioning about the brother's death and my trips to Saint Lucy's Grotto but never giving up on my quest for an answer!

31

A Search for Answers and a Solution

 I finally find a doctor who could fix what three operations could not make right. He was in a great hospital down in Manhattan known for these types of injuries. Finally, an answer, but it came with a catch. You see the doctor told me that there are two ways of going about it. First he said he could put a halo around the knee and that I would have to turn four screws every day until the bone grew and made the knee straight, but the only problem with that was I would be out a year. I told the doctor that I would like more opinions. I want to get back to work right away within reason. He told me he could do the osteotomy all over again. I asked him how long it would take to have it heal so I could get back to work. He told me six months. I told him to let's do it. So now I am faced with the same operation all over again to fix what didn't work the first three times. I was faced with the same chances of infection and a high rate of complications. I told him I was set. Another trip to Saint Lucy's Grotto and more prayers and more holy water to bathe the knee.

 The FDNY doctor was all ready for my next step towards my goal of getting back to the firehouse. The doctor had set up a time on a Friday for the operation. I head down to the hospital, parked my car at the firehouse in the Bronx and took a cab down to the hospital. I get to the hospital check-in and the nurses prep me for my next journey on getting back to work. They stick me with the IV. I get a gown, and they come in and shave the leg and have me sign the knee that was going to be operated on. You wonder why they need to do it when the left leg looked like a jigsaw puzzle with all the fresh scars. Turns out that would be the least of my problems. So I am ready to go! After an hour of waiting, the nurse comes in and says, "Mr. Edwards I am sorry, but we cannot do the operation today because the doctor doesn't have enough help for the operating room." I said, "He needs help?" She told me he had to do a lot of bone work. I am thinking to myself... What the hell is going on? Is this the message I was asking for? Was God telling me not to do it? Well even if God did tell me not to do it, I would have to disobey him because no one was going to stand in my way to get back to fighting the red devil! So I get dressed, and they disconnect me from the IV and then the doctor walks in and says, "Chris, I need more people in the operating room because it's going to take some time and I have to take bone off of your hip for a graft. Call me Monday and we can set up an appointment for next week." I walked out of the hospital and grabbed a cab back up to the Bronx. When I got into the firehouse, the brothers couldn't believe that they canceled the operation. They were joking that the fire department didn't pay their bill from the last one. We all got a good laugh from all of this. I went home and had some time to think about it. I still was going to get it done. My mission was not complete. I still had more to give, no matter what obstacles got in my way. Well, little did I know there were going to be a lot of obstacles in my way in the upcoming days, weeks, months and year.

DING! DING! Round two. I head to the hospital, and the nurse says it feels like you never left. I laughed and said, "Do we have everyone today?" They said yes we even brought in extra, and we all laughed. You see I wasn't mad at the false alarm the last time; I just figured it was the way it was supposed to be, but now I am ready and so was everyone else. When I came to, I remember getting sick and thinking here we go again... another overnight. When the doctor came in to see me, he wanted me to stay an extra night so they could watch for any signs of infection. I got a room with a young guy. His name was Ray, who had been in a bad car accident years ago and never had his legs fixed. They were badly deformed from a car crash that left him paralyzed from the waist down. Ray and I got along great. We had a lot in common. We talked about sports and me being a firefighter, but most of all we talked about God. You see he told me after the accident he was on the verge of committing suicide, but he prayed to God and after a while he was able to feel everything from his waist up and had the feeding tube removed when he was in the hospital after the accident. You see he had a strong belief in God and the power of prayer. I told him about my travels and operation; nowhere near what Ray had gone through but in my own way, a struggle. We talked about family, and we both were in troubled relationships. His girlfriend walked out on him after he was paralyzed. I told him about the abusive relationship I was in. Ray couldn't understand how people who can walk and talk and get up to make their beds and go for walks be so unhappy. I thought about what he had said, and it really did make a lot of sense. I learned a lot with Ray, my roommate. After a day, the doctor told me he wanted me to stay a few more days because I had a slight fever. He said he was going to put me on some antibiotics. Ray had been on them for a few days before I came into the room. The next day the doctor told me that the fever didn't break and that he was going to move me to a private room. It overlooked the East River. They put me in the room, and I said goodbye to a friend that I figured I would never see again. I still pray for you Ray...hoping they fixed your legs so someday you can play basketball again. What was supposed to be a few days stay, ended up being two and half weeks again! The infection was pretty bad. They had me on two powerful IV antibiotics, but I made the best of my stay. The nurses were great. You see I had another Foley catheter in when I got in the private room that they were going to take it out, but the only thing was there was this pretty young nurse taking care of me and me sure as hell didn't want her to take it out. The doctor ordered to have it removed before another infection could start. I said to myself I have to think quickly. When she came in, she deflated the balloon inside the bladder and had to get something and said she would be right back. When she left the room, I grabbed the tube and slowly pulled it out! She walked back in the room and was shocked to see I had already done it. She said, "You are crazy!" How did you know I deflated the balloon? I told her I just had it done a few months ago, and I watched the nurses. I told her about my stays, and she said, "I am going to have to keep an eye on you, and walked out laughing. "You see in the next 2 1/2 weeks, I got to know them all. What a great bunch of caring people in the hospital. The brothers were coming to visit and would bring me good food, Italian combo's, beans and rice, Chinese food, cannolis, and cookies. I had more food, and I would share it with the nurses. I would call the kids every night to tell them goodnight and that I loved them.

I had been in there for two weeks when a friend came to visit, and it was getting late and I didn't want her to walk up the street late at night. I told her I would walk her up to the corner that was a block away from the hospital. She said you could not do that. I said watch. I unscrewed the IV, put on a robe and walked towards the elevator and asked the nurses if they needed anything from the corner store. They just laughed and said, "Yes could you get me a cold drink?" Then they laughed. I walked around to the elevator with my crutches and got in and headed down to the first floor and up the block and waited for the bus and then said goodbye to her laughing the whole way calling me crazy. I walked back in, got into the elevator and walked up to the nurse's desk and said, "Here is your cold drink." They were shocked and said, "Where did you get this?" I told you I was going to the corner for the papers and drink. They hesitated for a minute and laughed and said, "Yea right you walked up to the corner." I laughed and walked to my room and two days later, I was released from the hospital thinking I would be on my way back to the firehouse, but the year was only going to get worse, not physically but mentally and emotionally...

32

Seeing the Sunlight through the Clouds

It was a bittersweet feeling getting out of the hospital. I had made so many friends, from the nurses to Ray and other patients that I had met during my two and a half weeks stay. It was a breath of fresh air, walking out and getting into a cab and heading up to the firehouse to get my car. When I got there, the brothers were sitting at the kitchen table waiting to present me with a plaque. The kitchen is where you get no sympathy! They will bust your balls, but if it's anyone's family, they would be the first ones to step up to help. Well, one of the brothers went out of his way to get a cow knee bone and cut it, put screws, nails, hook up metal springs and metal brackets into the bone to represent my knee. He even went as far as to put my name on the plaque and a medical description of the operations. They were teasing me about getting three operations upstate. They said, "What veterinarian did your operations?" Then another brother would say, "Yea the same one that neutered his dog." This was a sign of love, believe it or not. People on the outside just don't get the firehouse humor that only firemen get. They made lunch for me and even had a cake saying, "Bite Me" ... Lol. I will not describe the picture on the cake, but I will leave it up to you... just think! Crazy Firemen humor and you will get the picture. There is something about the firehouse and the brothers that gave me hope and a great feeling of relief that all the operations were over, and I was on my way back!

I had a visit to my doctor a couple of weeks later, and he said the bone graft looked good. It was just a matter of time before I could start physical therapy so I decided to drive to Florida on my new knee. I was walking with a cane when I left New York. When I got down to Florida, it was like a miracle. I got a hotel on the beach and would walk the beach in the morning. Within a day, I was walking without pain or the cane! It was like charging the battery of a rechargeable flashlight. I had a brighter looking future than I had four operations ago. I was heading to a full recovery. I spent about a week down in Florida, and when I headed back home, I decided my first stop would be St. Lucy Church for some more prayers. I was feeling pretty good in the daytime, but the night was a different story. You see the doctor opened up both sides of my knee. He put two four-inch metal plates on both sides of my knee, screwing them in with eight screws four on each side and bone from my hip and placed it between the bones for the graft. It had been about two months, and the surgeon gave me the "Ok" for therapy. He said I should do three days a week. I had another appointment with the FD doctor, and she was very happy to see that it was looking positive for a comeback. She gave me the authorization for the therapy and now the painful reminder of the four operations came crashing back. It was very painful, but the prize outweighed the pain. It was intense! Moving the leg in ways to try and prevent the scar tissue from building up around the knee and to prevent it from freezing up.

Well, I had a lot of time to reflect on my future and my life. Every chance I had between running back and forth to therapy, I would see my children upstate and my grandson out in Missouri. My oldest son was going to the Culinary Institute and was graduating in July. He had worked so hard, and I was very proud of him. I told him to take the fire department test because when you are a great cook, firehouses will fight over you, especially when your father was a brother. So some things in my life were looking up, but my personal life was like a tornado wreaking havoc, giving me stress. You see trying to please everyone and needing to take care of myself first had me feeling guilty. It always seems that the good times only last for a short time when you are a firefighter because at any given time your life could end! Even in life, you are always waiting for the next fire!

The firehouse was going well. I would stop by there in the morning on my way to therapy and bring in bagels and cream cheese for breakfast. I would have my cup of coffee and sit at the kitchen table and enjoy hearing all the ball busting! Laughter was a big part of my recovery, without it, I don't think I could have made it back. The brothers told me we were getting a new probie during the night tour, so I made sure I came back to meet the kid. I got in before the probie did and I was glad to see a friend named Matt. Matt was a guy who I had invited into the firehouse a few years before. He lived down the block from the firehouse in a special home for mentally challenged adults. He loved being around the brothers and being in the firehouse. He was welcomed by all the brothers. This helped him feel better and loved. He would take the bus to the factory he worked at. It was just something for him to do. The pay wasn't much but when he got paid one day the attendant from the home came to firehouse asking about his money. Apparently, when he got paid they would save it for him, and he came home one day with nothing in his pocket. We told the attendant he hadn't been there that day. The next day Matt came by, and I asked him what happened to his money. He said he gave it to his girlfriend, who worked at a bar. Some of the brothers heard it and asked him what he was doing in a bar. He said he puts his money on top of the bar like everyone else, and his girlfriend takes it. We asked him if he was allowed to drink. He told us no and that he drank soda. Which gave us the clue that someone is taking his money. Well, a couple of the brothers knew the bar and went over to talk to the owner. That was the end of him going into the bar and the end of the bartender (girlfriend). Well, Matt would love to dress up like an officer and now we have this probie coming in. So that day he put on the officer's uniform, and we told him about the probie. We told him to question him and straighten him out about the rules of the firehouse. Well, the door opens and in walks this young guy with his uniform and he introduces himself as Firefighter Gorumba. The brothers don't give the probie a chance, and they are all over him. They turn around and into the room walks Matt. He starts screaming that the kitchen needs to be mopped, and his waste paper basket wasn't empty. He looks at the probie and says, "What are you looking at, grab the mop!" So the probie grabs the mop and starts cleaning the floor. We are all laughing our asses off. Matt is loving the attention and being able to boss the probie around. Well, Matt looked at the clock and told us he had to go home. He took the shirt off and walked out the door. All awhile the kid is still mopping. Finally, we let the probie in on the joke, and he was laughing his ass off! This probie would play a big part in my life. He was a great guy who came over from the NYC sanitation and always wanted to be a NYC firefighter. He fit right in and had no problem cleaning the first night. He did everything a probie was supposed to do and more. He had a wife who was pregnant with his first child, a boy.

Well, as I mentioned, I have learned a lot about life during this job, and my plan to get back to the firehouse was looking good. On the days I could, I would go to Arthur Avenue in the Bronx, a big Italian neighborhood that had unbelievable food on every block. When I wasn't in the firehouse, I was at the market eating at Cafe al Mercato. I would go there for lunch and sometimes breakfast. I would sit there and was welcomed to sit at the table with the owner and friends while his sons ran the counter. Here you would get real Italian food made from recipes from their mother and grandparents from their homeland. I became friends with a great group of people; friends I am close with to this day. This is all part of the positive mindset I needed to get back. I would sit there and listen to the stories of the way Arthur Ave used to be. How much has the area changed since the early 60's? You could get fresh sweet or hot sausages, made by two brothers and before them made by their mom and dad, homemade mozzarella cheese, homemade ravioli by a family that owned it for 100 years, fresh baked bread, the best in the city...pastry shops, cannoli's. I was in heaven! Thank God I had physical therapy because I would have been 300 pounds! On 187th street is a church Our Lady of Mt. Carmel. I would spend many days praying in that beautiful church. I became friends with store owners who today I call friends. I have to thank them for their moral support. They don't know it, but they played a big part in my comeback to the job I loved the most!

33

The Good, the Bad and the Sad....

Things were going good after the little break
from all the rat race and the aches and pain of
the northeast weather. The therapy was painful
but the reward was well worth it. Things looked
to be going well with the recovery, full speed
ahead. There was a new probie in the house
and a couple of transfers from good companies.
The firehouse was busy and the new brothers
were fitting in well. Father's day was coming up.
It was always a tough day for me. See when my
dad passed away 23 years ago, I forgot to buy
him a Father's day card. It was the first time
that happened for as long as I could remember.
Since my father died in 1992, I would always
make sure I visited the cemetery. I would bring
a folding chair and sit there and have a talk with

my father, clean his tombstone and place flowers on his grave. Carnations were my father's favorite flowers, so I would place a bunch next to his WWII plaque. I would tell him how the rehab for the knee was going. All along knowing that he was by my side in spirit helping me through the tough times. This was the way I would celebrate Father's day.

It was June 17, 2001, Father's day fell on a Sunday that year. My routine was to pick up my sons and take them to church and bring them over to the cemetery to visit their grandfather. Church was over, and I headed to the flower shop for my bunch of carnations when I hear on the radio that there was a bad fire in Long Island City in Queens. Knowing that anything could happen, I said a prayer that all the brothers would be safe and no one hurt as I set up my chair and said my prayers and talked to my father. We sat there for about half an hour. I had to get them back to the house since they had school on Monday. I dropped them off and gave them a kiss and told them I would give them a call on Monday when they got home from school. I turned the radio on as I drove down back to the Bronx. Now I hear on the radio that two firefighters are seriously injured. My heart dropped to my stomach, thinking that this couldn't be happening on Father's day. I called the brothers and asked them if they heard anything on the job. They told me that two of the brothers were in the hospital, and the other brother was trapped in the basement and had made a radio transmission for the brothers to come and get him!! You see no one understands what's it's like to hear a brother trapped and not be able to reach him. The feeling of when the radio goes silent, and you are nowhere near reaching the trapped brother. The job was in a general hardware store. Rescue companies from Queens had responded to the job and were trying to force the door when a series of explosions occurred. The force was so powerful it knocked down brothers in the street. It caused a wall to collapse on them, trapping them underneath bricks and other debris. The other brother was inside and the floor gave way and he ended up being trapped in the basement while calling for help. The Job reached a 5th alarm. The death toll was three firefighters dead on Father's day! This was another loss that's hard to explain on a day we celebrate our fathers. Now you look at these brothers, and you know that they had children, as a matter of fact the brothers killed that day, two of them had three children each, and the other brother had two children, leaving a total of eight fatherless children and three widows. The youngest of the eight being 3 and the oldest was 12 years old. Now this was one of the worst years in the history of the New York City Fire Dept. for line of duty deaths on the job. The feeling at the firehouse was as low as I have ever seen in my career. It was not just the loss of the brothers but the day that it happened was a stab in the heart. We waited for the four sets of five bells to sound. The fire service is rich with ceremony, custom, and tradition. The custom of rendering final honors has its origins in the fire department of the city of New York, where many years ago, long before the advent of radios or pagers, fire alarms, and daily announcements were dispatched from central headquarters to outlying firehouses by a system of bell commands and telegraph. These bells are the way we show respect and honor for these heroes. The next few days I questioned how God could allow this to this happen? I really never got an answer, but I felt these things are not caused by God but by evil. The next couple of days we were getting set up for the funerals. The brothers killed, that unforgettable day, one of the worst days in the history of the fire department were all under the age of 50. The emotional feelings that you go through as a firefighter when you attend a brother's funeral is a strange thing because you feel hurt and sadness for the brother, his wife, children, family, his friends, and the brothers that shared the memories and the laughs on the job with him. Then when the wake and the funeral are over with, you celebrate the brother's life. When a firefighter dies, whether it's at a fire or when they are at home, you always take care of his family. There is a brother who steps up and helps out his family. If it's off the job, sometimes collections are made to help the cost of the funeral, if it is needed. Food is brought to the family. Their kids may need rides or other kinds of assistance to help out his family. Then at the funeral, full military-style honors are presented. The respect are the honor guards at the head and feet of the casket. Standing at attention every member of his company would take his turn at the casket. This is done by his company and other brothers who were friends with him will also ask to be a part of the honor guards. The two brothers that died were from Rescue 4, which is an elite group of firefighters with many fields of experience. They are brought in to perform searches and have high-tech equipment to fight fires inside closed walls and to perform other lifesaving maneuvers. The other brother killed that day was from Ladder 163. This fire was started when two teenagers were playing behind the hardware store; they accidently knocked over a can of gas which made its way into the basement of the store and when the water heater turned on it ignited the gas causing the fire. The explosions were caused by other flammable liquids stored in the hardware store. These are the hidden dangers we face every day as a firefighter...the unknown.

The companies in our battalion put together a bus to attend the funeral. It was a packed with brothers from other firehouses in our area of the Bronx. Our probie was on the bus. Here is a young man starting his career off, seeing the death of three firefighters and attending their funerals. I was wondering what could be going through his mind. Later I would find out. There is also an unwritten rule that no one outside your firehouse could abuse your probie (bust his balls). Well, that day we were on our way to the funeral, and there was a cooler of beverages on the bus for some brothers to help them take away some of their pain or try to numb the thought that this could happen to anyone of us at any time. After an emotional funeral where you have seen the widow and their children and a child carrying his father's helmet, it puts a knot in your stomach and tears in your eyes. Even I had a beverage on the way back to the coalition. A celebration of the brother's lives where we all go after the mass and the burial is over to hear the stories of the brothers who have passed away. You laugh, you hear stories that choke you up, and what a great guy they were. It puts thoughts in your mind that we are all alike. We are made from the same cloth. We all have the same love for the job and the

222

brothers we work and live with. Even though they were from Queens and I never worked with them, I felt like I could tell the same stories I heard just using the different names of brothers I worked with because we all have it in our heart and mind to help people. The trip back to the firehouse was a memorable one. The cooler was in the back of the bus, and if anyone wanted a drink the probie would have to go back and get it for them. Only guys in our house could tell him to get one so every time he was asked to go to the cooler, we would smack his ass and scream like a cowboy riding a horse. Yeah! Yeah! Every time he got up it was a gauntlet. The whole bus was laughing, and the probie was laughing back and forth to the cooler. See I told him what I learned when I first got on the job, always laugh and never let them see it bothers you. The kid passed the test with flying colors. A few days after the wake I spoke to him about his feeling on the death of the three brothers, and he told me, "Chris I have been waiting my whole life to become a firefighter. I understand the risks that I take when I took this job, but this is my dream, and I will never let my dream go! I looked at him and told him I knew how he felt and that I stand right along side him. I told him he did the right thing on the bus. He laughed and said he had a great time getting his ass beat. We both laughed... as I left to go to therapy to get my ass beat to get back to the job we loved the most- the firehouse. One month later that great young firefighter and father to be would be transferred back to his firehouse in Staten Island. A place he called home, where his dreams were being realized as a New York City firefighter. One month later he would die on the job from a massive heart attack at a fire in Staten Island, August 28, 2001. Twenty-eight years young, a baby on a way, beautiful wife, a dream to become a firefighter. From the wake to the funeral, the honor guards, his company took the lead with the honor guards and the help with his family. Later his wife would say to me that he had the greatest time working in Engine 81 in the Bronx. It brought tears to my eyes that I still cry today. God bless your soul brother.

I would continue to question God and the things that were going on around me in my life. At one point, I kept thinking it might be me, like a jinx or something, but fifteen days later I would see more evil than anyone could ever imagine!!

34

A Day Grown Men Cried

For the next fifteen days, I can say I really don't remember very much. I was numb after attending the wake and the funeral for the Probie during the days that followed his tragic death. I remember the brothers in the firehouse were still mourning, but we laughed and talked about the good times we shared with him and the bus ride for the brothers of the Father's day fire. As we talked about the great time we had with him, one of the brothers brought up the fact that life is too short, and some people just don't understand what it's all about. I certainly did, all the loss was wearing very heavy on my soul. The visits to St. Lucy slowed down. My faith had taken a beaten the last year, but my motivation to get back was in full stride.

Nothing was going to stop me. I was determined to get back. I had a doctor's appointment the second week of September on the thirteenth. The FDNY doctor was in only on Monday and Tuesday, so when she saw me she told me to take two weeks, and she would see me on the week of the 17th of September with a possibility of going on light duty (desk job). I was on my way back! Now the therapy was going well. I had a doctor's appointment in Rockland County at 11:00 am to see another orthopedic specialist. The day was September 11, 2001. I got up early that day to get on the road. When I got up, I looked out the window and thought to myself how perfect the day was. The boys caught the school bus, and I got ready to take a shower. I put the television on and seen the trade center was on fire. I changed the channel to hear the news report that said a plane had just crashed into the Trade Center in downtown Manhattan. I looked and thought about the private jets I would see fly low under the George Washington Bridge on clear days. I knew there were going to be thousands of casualties and that we were going to lose a firefighter fighting that fire. See high-rise fires are tough, but building over a hundred stories with the amount of fire I saw on the newscast, we were definitely going to lose a brother. I prayed that it wouldn't turn out that way, but as I turned to get in the shower, I heard the reporter scream another plane just crashed into the south tower of the Trade Center!! Right then and there I knew that it was a terrorist attack! I felt sick to my stomach because now I knew for sure we would have a large number of casualties of civilians, firefighters, and other first responders. I skipped the shower and got in the car heading to the firehouse. As I drove down, I grabbed the rosary beads on my rear view mirror and prayed!   I prayed that maybe we didn't lose anybody and that the buildings were empty, but in my heart I knew it had to be an unbelievable number of deaths and injured. I had the radio on and was searching the channels for more information. I put on the Howard Stern show and heard the seriousness of their voices. The whole crew was silent and in shock; they were trying to get more details of the attack. People were calling in down near the Trade Center describing what they had seen and who they thought was responsible for the attacks. Then I heard that all the planes around the country have been directed to land and get out of the sky. Well at that time I heard that a plane just crashed into the Pentagon in Washington DC. I called my son's mother and told her about the attack. She was at work, and I told her to pick the boys up from school because there were more planes in the air and their school wasn't too far from West Point Military Academy. She told me that they would be alright. I wanted to turn around, but I knew I had to get to my firehouse and get down to the Trade Center to help out. As I was heading down, the unbelievable happened. The South Tower, the second tower hit, had just collapsed. I started crying and sobbing, still holding the rosary beads praying for the victims and the brothers. Praying that all the brothers were safe. I was driving by the hospital where I had the appointment, I figured I would stop in and tell the doctor that I couldn't see him and had to get to the firehouse. I pulled up to the hospital, and there was a line of people donating blood for the survivors. As I ran into the hospital, all the pain seems to leave my knee, and the adrenaline had kicked in. I went

229

over to the nurse and told her my name and said, I am a New York City Firefighter, and I have to leave and cancel my appointment. She told the doctor and he brought me into his office and said he had a friend who is a firefighter. He told me his name and asked if I could find out if he was safe. I left his office, and he said God Bless you and be safe. I told him, "Doc say a prayer." I left walking by the line which, had doubled in size. I got into my car and put the radio on to get road info. The news channel said all bridges heading into the city were closed. I thought, great how am I going to get there. I got back on the quickway and there were cars pulled over on the side of the roads. I see an unmarked cop car with his light flashing, I pulled up to him showing him my badge and he screamed for me to follow him. We were heading to the Tappan Zee Bridge. I have always said a prayer going over the bridge for a good friend who had jumped off it, back in the Eighties. I would say a prayer for all the people who had passed away in my lifetime every time I crossed it. There was only a handful of names, who were very important to me. Later that "List of Names" was going to grow by a large number. The cop was driving in and out of traffic and on the shoulder and the grass. On the way down dodging traffic, I hear Howard Stern report that the North Tower just collapsed! I prayed out loud, not knowing what it had looked like as I was saying my prayers to all the loved ones I lost crossing the Tappan Zee. I looked to the South and could see the smoke climbing into the sky. When we reached the toll booth, the collectors looked like they were in shock. I saw a woman in the booth as we drove by and she just waved, no questions asked, I felt she knew where we were heading. The last toll was the Yonkers toll; it was the same there. They just waved us through, seeing the police car and a car with FDNY plaque in the front window they had to have said a prayer as we drove by. I knew I was praying the whole way down. I cannot remember the speed we were traveling, but I remember passing fire trucks from all over the state and other local fire companies from around the state. There were police cars and ambulances heading down towards the towers of smoke. When we got to the firehouse exit, I beeped my horn and waved. I wish I could have given the officer a hand shake and a hug, but I said a silent prayer for his safety. I got off the exit, and I could see the firehouse. It was surrounded by fire trucks from all over the Bronx and Yonkers. They even had volunteer companies from upstate responding to help out. It was a State of Emergency, a complete shutdown of New York City. I parked my car, and I could still feel that sick feeling in my stomach, knowing that someone I knew was possibly dead.

All the brothers met me with a hug and a few tears trying to make sense of what had just happened. I remember sitting at the kitchen table trying to figure who might be working down in Manhattan that day. We all ran through names, and there were a few guys who transferred to Manhattan companies who had worked with us in our firehouse. I went up to the house watchman and took the members phone number list and called the brothers that knew were in Manhattan. Every phone call, I prayed that I would get a return call telling me that the brother was ok, but I never received a call back that day or night or ever. The calls were to brothers who were working that day. I would find out they all died. Six numbers, no call backs. The firehouse was packed with firefighters from all over the Tri-State Area (NY, NJ, PA, and CT). We talked about who could have done this, and I think we all agreed that it was the same group of Radical Islamic terrorists that tried to blow up the Trade center in February 1993. After that bombing, the fire department decided to train us in a crash course on terrorist attacks. It was a one-day class just a basic course to tell us if you are a first responder to a terrorist attack, you would be considered a casualty because first responders and innocent civilians are their targets. They look for a large body count of fatalities. They also have two means of attack that are separated about 10 to 15 minutes apart. First attack targets civilians and then the second is for first responders. Knowing that, it didn't make me feel any better when the South Tower came down because I knew it would be filled with Firefighters, police officers, and EMT'S. We all wanted to get down there and help out, but the officers were waiting for an order from the upper echelon of the fire department. The problem was they were all killed in the attacks. After the towers came down, the brothers and the brass (leaders of the FDNY) were missing. So the chain of command had to be established. We waited in the firehouse preparing for the worst but praying for the best. The kitchen table was a whirlpool full of anger, prayers, worries, tears, hugs and reassuring wives that their husbands were ok, but we really had no idea. See Firemen help, we have all the answers, and we stand up in the face of danger. We put our life on the line every day.

35

Steps Away from Reality

Time seem to drag by; then the first wave of brothers who were sent down there in the morning started coming back and told stories of things they had witnessed. It just made me want to get down there as soon as I could. One of the brothers told us that they were around the Trade Center when they felt the ground rumble and people started screaming to get out of the way because building Number 7 is collapsing. He said he felt like he was running for his life which actually he was. I thought to myself that if he felt that way about a forty- seven story building, how the other brothers must have felt about 100 stories. They must have felt helpless. We greeted them with hugs. They were contacting their families to tell them that they were safe. I could hear one brother crying on the phone and saw him wipe tears from his eyes. They told us about rigs (Engines and Trucks) on fire and twisted steel from the North and South Towers all around the West Side Highway. They told us there was a large pieces of steel that took off the corner of the financial building and cut right through it like a hot knife going through a stick of butter. They were speechless about the bodies of the victims and brothers they seen laying in the street covered in white dust from the debris cloud that covered downtown Manhattan.

As they were telling the story, two NYC Correction buses pulled up to quarters. One of the brothers came and said that the prisoners in green jumpsuits were taking out trays of food and were setting up tables on the apparatus floor. We all went in to help out. I was shocked to see that they brought in baked chicken and bread, mashed potatoes, vegetables, drinks, and dessert. For a minute, it was a diversion from what we had just heard. I remember thinking to myself that this is the way life should be-everyone joining in to help out in times of trouble.

I tried to eat something because I didn't know when I would be able to get something to eat. Then all of a sudden we hear the computer go off! It was sending the names of all the MIA (missing in action). The list was names of all the brothers that were officially working. These were the brothers on the riding list for the houses that responded to the Trade Center during the first plane attack and the second attack in the South Tower. There were hundreds of brothers that were on the computer printout. Looking at the names made me sick to my stomach. Names of guys I had worked with and even guys that I had called earlier in the day. I could only imagine the devastation that awaited us in lower Manhattan, but the reality of the attack just became real personal. We wouldn't know the true amount of brothers, police officers and other first responders killed because other brothers got off their tours in the morning and jumped on the rigs heading down to the help out. They would also become casualties.

36

Facing Reality

The drive to get down to the Trade Center to help out in the recovery was going to become somewhat of a problem. There was a city-wide announcement that all New York City firefighters should go home and report back at 9 am for their morning tour. I said to myself, *"What the hell are they sending us home for?"* This made no sense to me or a few of the other brothers. We were like*, go home and come back in the morning? What about all the people trapped? What about the brothers that are missing?* Going home for me was not an option. I had to get down there one way or another. Then I thought... wait a minute... I'm getting ready to go on light duty. I don't have to be in for my tour. So

239

around 10 pm, Engine 13 from Yonkers was called to respond down to the Trade Center. They were riding with a chief and his aid. The engine had four guys and were taking two brothers from our house with them to help them out. I see my chance to get down there, and this was it. I asked the chief from Yonkers if I could catch a ride down with them. He said yes and that he was not real sure of where to go so I could help him out. Bingo! There it was. They rounded everyone up from the companies, and we were on our way. Before we left, some of the brothers came over to me and asked how the hell I was going to walk around down there with two metal plates and eight screws in my knee. I told them I would find a way! On the way down there you could feel the tension in the rig from everyone. I think it was because of the unknown. Not knowing what we were going to see and what we might find was the real reason for the tension. In my head, all the names and faces of the brothers missing were playing in my head like a movie projector. Thinking of who made it and who didn't was something that was killing me on the inside.

This was a mission, and I had hopes of finding them all alive and well. The closer we got to the Trade Center, you could see a glow from the light towers that were hooked up to a generator and the smoke that was still rising from the fires. There was burning in and around the twisted steel beams that would later be called the Pit, the Hole, and Ground Zero. We drove down the West Side Highway, and as soon as we crossed over where the Bronx meets Manhattan, you could smell a distinct odor, like a musty smell that later I could never get out of my mind... that scent or smell. The closer we got to Ground Zero you could see a white powder covering everything, cars, trees, sidewalks, store windows. It was like a frost. As we got closer, the powder-like covering became deeper and covered everything you could see, and the smell became stronger. Now it was mixed with the smell of smoke. On some of the windows of cars and stores were the words, *"God Bless Our City"*, *"God Bless America"*. We got down to a command center that was set up on Church Street. There were companies from all over the city and the Tristate area.

The chief from Yonkers reported into the Chief in Charge. I knew the Chief from the Bronx. I had worked for him when he was a captain... good guy. I went over to him and told him that we had three guys from the Bronx with the Yonkers Company, and if there was any way we could get into the hole and help out with the search? He told me that there were companies ahead of us and that when he could he would. So now all there was to do was wait and think and take it all in. You could see papers in the trees and women's shoes in the six inches of powder. Not knowing if it was from someone running to get away or from someone who had jumped from the towers. I saw fully armed soldiers following behind in military vehicles. It was something out of movie set. It was so much to take in, and the thought of victims, friends, brothers, just down the street from where we were standing was too much. I went back over to the Chief and asked again, "Chief anything yet?" He told me he didn't want to give me the crappy job of stripping (taking all tools and hoses off of wrecked trucks and engines) Rigs. Just then another chief came in to relieve him. I thought that we would never get in to help with the search. This chief was from Brooklyn, and I went up to him and asked again. It seemed like I went up every half hour. Finally, this chief said to go over to the Post Office and relieve the company hitting pockets of fire on building number seven. He gave me the radio, and I went back and told the chief from Yonkers we got a job. We are on our way. When we started towards the post office, every step you took would cause the white powder to make a dust cloud as we all walk. Then another armored vehicle drove by and it looked like fog in the morning rising off of hot pavement. Everything was being run by generators. We needed flashlights to find our way into the post office because there was no electric in the building. We walked by the mail sorting bins and there was dust all over the inside of the building. Mail was still in the slots and mail in trays. It looked like time just froze, and all the people ran out and left things right where they were standing and ran for their lives. We made it up to the floor where the brothers were operating the line; it was out a large window. You could stand up and hit the pockets of fire. Almost all the windows of building number seven had fire blowing out of them. I went to take the knob from the company we were relieving and this young guy from the Bronx, with a year on the job, said," I got the knob!" I grabbed it from him and said, "No I got the knob!" I told him, "Kid you are just starting your career, I am fighting to stay." He handed me the line and backed me up. As I was hitting pockets of fire, I could hear this high pitched noise and knew right away what it was from. PASS device (Personal Alert Safety System) that sounds an alarm off when a firefighter is in trouble. The alarm goes off when there is no movement for 15 to 30 seconds. The more I listened, the more I heard. It sounded like a pond on a warm summer night with small frogs making a high pitched peeping sound. I knew then that we lost a lot of brothers because these only go off when a firefighter is not moving. I turned to the two brothers from the Bronx and said we have to get in and help with the search. They agreed. I gave the radio to the chief from Yonkers and said we have to get in there and look for our brothers. He shook my hand, and we walked out and up Church Street. When we turned the corner, we saw the pile... totally devastating! I will never forget that smell and the sight of that day. Now our work had just begun....

37

Hope, a Four Letter Word that Carried Me

The sound of the PASS alarms was a haunting reminder that we had a lot of casualties. We walked up Church Street. The sun was rising on a new day. We came upon a scene that just didn't seem real. There were office papers in trees and also covering the streets all around Ground Zero. I thought to myself, "People who died must have had them in their hands when the planes attacked the towers". I looked around and there were shoes littering the streets, some with blood stains. There were articles of clothing mixed in with all the white dust. As we walked to the hotel across from what once was the largest buildings in the world, I saw a line of guys lined up double all the way to what looked like the Plaza. I could see a sphere that was 25 feet tall in the distance. It looked like a rolled up piece of aluminum. It was still there, a sign of hope. I figured if that could make it with all this steel and debris around it, then maybe some of the brothers and victims found ways to survive. There was an odor and I knew right away what it was, but in my mind I didn't want to admit it to myself, but it was the smell of death. I had smelled this odor many times before, and that odor would never go away. It was only going to get worse. The three of us were trying to get in with a search team. As I looked at the line, I saw a chief that I knew standing in the street giving guys a hand setting up search teams. I went over to him and shook his hand. I asked him what was going on with this line that went about three hundred yards out to what seemed to be the drop-off. He told me that they are working on a NYC Port Authority Cop, who was trapped for over twenty hours. They just freed one of them, and they were working on another cop. I told him that he had to get us down there to help. He questioned how the hell I could get around with the metal plates and screws in my knee. I told him to let me give it a try; I cannot go home. He still wasn't sure on how I was going to do it. I turned to him and said, "Chief, you retired two months ago, and you are here." He smiled and said, "I guess there is nothing going to stop you." I told him he had that right. He told me to get the Stokes Basket, which is a basket that we use to transport injured patients. One of the brothers told me that he was heading towards the Bronx, so the two of us walked out towards the hole. There were guys from all walks of life lining both sides of this line to the end of the hole. I remember thinking that if we found two people alive, we have a good chance of finding others alive. As I walked, I was waiting for my knee to give out and snap. I had no faith in it holding up, but that adrenaline kicked in, and nothing was going to stop me. We get out to the end of the line, and now we are standing on the top of the pile. It was so high you couldn't see the Westside Highway. We were handing down tools into a hole where this officer had been trapped for more than twenty-four hours. They finally freed him from the rubble. Then after two long hours, we handed down the Stokes, and they strapped him in. I will never forget his face and what he asked me. He said he wanted to see his wife and kids. I looked him in the eye and said, *"Brother you are free! You are going home to your family."* I held his hand and for a moment and a great feeling of hope took over my body and mind. It was the answer I needed to hear!

As we watched the basket being carried with the officer in it, I felt that if he could survive so could other people. Knowing how firefighters are, I figured some of them could have made it out. I walked out of the hole and wondered where I should go. I walked up Church Street knowing that there was a firehouse, figuring that they might be gathering up brothers to form search teams. As soon as I walked up the street, all of a sudden I remembered that my knee had two metal plates and eight screws in it. I could feel the pain, like a burning feeling every step I took, but when I was at the edge of the hole, I felt no pain. I walked by police and firefighters and construction workers that were heading towards Ground Zero. A news reporter who I recognized from a local channel came up to me and asked me if he could interview me. I told him that I am not supposed to be here. I explained that my knee had plates and screws in it, and I couldn't do it. He said he understood and patted me on the back and said thank you. I walked up to the corner of Duane Street, and I see the firehouse was surrounded by firetrucks and firefighters meeting others that were just coming out from the pit. These were the brothers that worked in the house and others from around lower Manhattan. You could tell who was just coming into work and the others who were down there when the towers came down. They were covered in the white dust and had a lost look on their faces. There were hugs and tears of joy and sadness, but a lot of hope that we would find people and our brothers alive. I was surprised to see my company from the Bronx had been relocated to Manhattan. The brothers came over to me and asked me how it was, and I explained to them what we had done that night and early morning. I told them I have hope that we will find people alive in the hole. There were stories being told about people who rode down a piece of concrete from the eighty-third floor. There was that hope again!

I was standing watching all the brothers when I see these two guys with cameras and they were filming around the firehouse and the brothers in their moment of being reunited. I was mad at the thought of these two taking advantage of private moments of emotions between two brothers, but they were not being chased away, and I could see that they also had white dust on their clothing. Later, I would gain a lot of respect for those two guys with the cameras. I see my captain was working. He had two sons who were missing in the collapse that he couldn't locate. You could see the stress on his face and the worries in his heart. He said to me, *"What the hell are you doing here?"* I told him I had gotten on Engine 13 from Yonkers and had been in the hole that night. He said I should look for a light duty job because of my knee, and I told him I wasn't going to go home and sit around. You could tell he was mad. We were all on edge. We had friends, sons, daughters, brothers missing, the list was endless. Everyone's emotions were like a stick of dynamite just waiting for a match to light it. We were full of hate and loss. We are firefighters; things like this are not supposed to happen to us. The facts of some of the missing were being talked about, some of the brothers had to run for their lives as the buildings were coming down people were being killed. There were people jumping out the windows. They saw bodies lying in the streets. They said the command center for the FDNY got wiped out. We felt the loss even without the official count of dead. I was trying to figure a way to get back down to the West Side Highway. The brothers who came out of the hole told us that the most damage was there, and they felt there might be some survivors there because people were running for their lives. I prayed for a way to get down there, and it happened, like a miracle, someone called in smoke coming from the South Tower. Two, one hundred story buildings come down, and someone smells smoke. My company has to take the run in. The captain comes over to me and told me not to even think about getting on the rig. I said, "No problem Capt." He gets in the Engine, and I jump in the back with the brothers. They all asked if I was crazy and I told them no... *I was on a mission*!

They laughed. The Engine goes around the block and heads towards the address of the call in. The captain calls in a 10-92 (false alarm). I open the door and with all due respect, I didn't want to show up the Captain, but I had to help out in the search. I walked off the rig, and I hear him scream, "Edwards I told you to get a light duty job!" I turned around to him and said,*" I am on a mission!"* They drove away, and I looked up and seen the devastation and the magnitude of the damage. I started to lose some of the hope I had. There were fires burning around the site, I seen twisted steel and fire trucks crushed like little toys. As I walked closer to the wreckage, I see the damage to the financial center and a one-hundred-foot beam cutting through the lobby of the building. On the way down it hit the side of the building taking off a huge chunk of it. It really was like a hot knife cutting through a stick of butter. I see a number painted on a wall that says, "Ninety-Third Floor." Just then and there, I realized there were ninety-two floors below me. I looked around and had a helpless feeling, not knowing where to start. There were fires burning with brothers pouring water on them. I looked up and seen the remains of the Trade Center sticking straight up in the middle of the rubble. I thought to myself; we will never get this cleaned up. But I prayed that we would find more people alive......

38

With All Due Respect

With all due respect, I had an overwhelming
feeling looking around the remains of the Trade
Center from the West Side Highway. When you
looked down Church Street, the remains were
as far as you could see. The west side was
where most of the towers landed. I can
remember the smell and the heat coming up
from below the twisted steel beams. There
were groups of firefighters working throughout
the site. Some were on what we would call the
"bucket brigades" that were made up of
hundreds of rescue workers. This was a time
where a cop and a firefighter would work side
by side to search for victims; some coworkers,
friends, family members. We worked side by
side. It was a mission, and we all had one thing

in mind, to find people alive! I saw a group of brothers from Brooklyn and didn't know any of them, but it didn't matter. I get in with this group, and they had found a hole between a steel beams that dropped down about ten feet. There was a large steel beam across the top of it that crossed over the void like a bridge. In the hole, we found remains of victims. It was tough getting them up out of the hole. These remains consisted of only body parts that were spread around like a final resting spot for a large group of people. We all handled the remains with respect. It was unreal. It was like working in a massive grave site except there were no bodies, just parts. There was bodily fluid all over. I had gloves on, but there was no way of keeping yourself from getting it on your turnout coat. The heat in the hole made it even tougher to work because you were sweating and breathing in smoke from fires burning below. Most of the body parts came up with some article of clothing on. There were pants with the lower half of a body. None of this set in until a week or so after I got out of the hole. You were there, and you did whatever you had to do to give the loved ones of the victims' closure, all along hoping and praying you would find someone alive. I stayed with this group of brothers until we brought up all the remains we could find. Then they called for a rescue dog, and they brought the dog to the edge of the hole. As he passed me, the dog stopped and buried his nose in the white dust and picked something up. Not thinking anything of it, I see the dog start smelling around the top of the hole. This dog had on little boots, a cover for his paws because of all the sharp steel. One of the brothers picked up this piece of flashing steel where the dog stopped. Underneath it we saw the remains of a body. The spine, a few ribs and a pelvis. It was burnt, and you could hardly tell what it was until I picked it up; then we realized it was a body. The trainer of the dog took his finger and swept the dogs mouth and pulled out a piece of flesh. He placed it into the body bag with the spine. This is what we had to do. In the early days after the towers were hit, it was mostly large body parts. As the days went on, the remains became smaller. We cleaned out the hole of all the remains. The group I was with regrouped with their companies.

Now it was time to find another group and another hole of remains. Walking around was tough. It was like climbing "make shift" ladders while talking to other brothers, construction workers, and police officers. As the night grew dark, I started in the bucket brigades, but all along I couldn't imagine how someone could survive this. There were rumors about people riding down from the eightieth floor on a slab of concrete. I prayed that it was true, but the more I seen, the more I was losing faith. During the night, you would hear saws cutting steel and some PASS alarms going off. The sound was haunting. By this time, there were thousands of people from all professions. Search teams from around the country. It was hard to keep track of where these groups were working. The names of the missing started to come to life. Some of the brothers were asking around about brothers missing, and we would hear they were working, and that they lost their whole company. Now the loss started to sink in. Down to the bone, the hurt was something I had never felt before because of the number of brothers you knew. I had just heard about one of the brothers I called on Tuesday, the eleventh, and found out he was killed. I could feel the pain and anger started to well up in my heart, but as I turned around to cry, I heard someone call my name. *Chrissy!!* I look up and it was a brother who I had worked with in 42- Engine. It was one of the brothers on the list. I had seen his name earlier and prayed he was still alive. Donny!! We hugged and shed a few tears. Just then all my faith came back to me. Seeing him took those tears away for that moment. We looked at one another for a second or two, and we were glad we were both alright and wished each other continued safety. Afterward, we went our separate ways searching for our brothers and other victims.

When I got back to the line of buckets, I realized at this point we were moving pails of debris. I wondered how many people we might be standing on below us. In the middle of moving all these buckets, you would hear across the sixteen acres a brother scream, *"Quiet!!"* It would travel around Ground Zero. *Quiet, Quiet, Quiet!!* All the tools would shut down, and you could hear a pin drop. They would lower a microphone into a hole and listen for any noise or breathing from someone who might be trapped. During this time, I was praying that we would hear that someone was found, but it never happened. The night of the 12th was warm, and the fires still raged under the pile. Charged lines were hitting pockets of fire. You could see smoke rising to the heavens from the flood lights that were run by giant generators...

Loss of time... Minutes changed to hours, hours changed to days, days changed to weeks, and weeks turned to months. The time I spent down at Ground Zero was something that seemed to meld together like the steel I stood on. Working on the buckets and moving debris seemed to be all we did for days on end. I would find a group that had an idea where some companies were supposed to be and some of the areas where the victims ran. Monday into Tuesday, Tuesday into Wednesday and so forth. We were exhausted but didn't take a break. We dug with our hands, with garden tools, shovels. We had welders cutting steel beams to open a spot to search in voids of the collapse. At one point, I stood next to a twisted beam where you could see as far down as the eyes could go. There was a glow the color of cherry red, along with heat and smoke that traveled up the beam. I could feel the heat on my bunker gear, and it ran up my chest into my face. I remember thinking to myself that I could feel the years being taken away with each breath I took. It was like I was frozen for a few minutes! I tried to call my family, but no cell phones were working in the hole. It was early Thursday morning, and I had not been home since the attack. I decided to go back to the firehouse and try to wash off all the white dust, sweat, body fluids and the smell of smoke and death from my body. So early Thursday morning I climbed out of the hole and headed up to firehouse in the Bronx. I walked up Church Street and seen the damage to the street, firetrucks, police cars, and stores. This was the first time since the first day that I got a chance to see what it looked like.

While I was walking a police officer with a white shirt (officer) came over to me and said, "My young son's school made up some shirts, and my son wanted me to give it to a firefighter, a hero." He lifted the shirt up to show me what it said; *"We love you, you're doing an amazing job."* Just below that was a smiley face, and on the back the little boy wrote his name Chris D from old Bethpage. I told him I was honored, but I was no hero. I told him the real heroes are the ones who never came back. I told him I would take the shirt and thanked him and told him I was grateful and would cherish the gift forever. I told him to give his son a hug for me. He took a picture of us together. He gave me a handshake and a hug and told me to be safe, and God bless. I turned away, and the tears started to flow. Just to think that this little boy and his schoolmates were that moved to make these gifts was too much for me to take. I hitched a ride from one of the brothers. As we drove up the West Side Highway, there were thousands of people lining both sides of the street holding pictures of loved ones that were missing. I thought to myself, out of all the remains we handled, I hope we gave some family peace to know they got their loved ones back...some kind of closure. Some people were playing music and cheering and clapping for every vehicle that drove by. It was a great feeling knowing that we had the whole city praying and pulling for us. This was another reason to get back in the hole and search! I asked the brother if he could drop me off at a church on Columbus Avenue and West 60th Street, Church of St. Paul the Apostle. I went inside, and the church was packed with people praying. Some were doing the rosary in groups of twenty. It was so moving, and I started to feel that five and four letter word coming back into my heart...hope and faith! I sat in a pew all by myself trying to avoid contact with people, but people came up to me and said they were sorry for my loss. I was shocked to hear that because I didn't want to believe they were lost. I still had faith we would find people!

39

Tension and Handshakes

This day really stood out in my mind because it's like the world stood still. Here it was a Thursday, a work day, and the church was packed with people praying. I think we all were looking for answers on how God could let this happen. Later, I would learn never to question God. I was full of anger, hurt and loss. This is why I had to stop in church early Thursday morning. I headed up to the firehouse in the Bronx. When I got there, I figured I would take a shower and head back down. It was the first time I got to talk to my family and friends. They were all worried about me. I reassured them that I was ok, and I would be safe. They didn't ask me what it looked like or what we were doing. I was glad because I had those horrible visions in the back of my mind, but I was trying not to think about them. I also was keenly aware that it was going to get worse. The brothers were all huddled around the kitchen table. A tornado of anger, helplessness, hurt and loss was swirling around the firehouse. You could cut the tension with a knife. Word was just coming in about the known deaths of firefighters, some brother's children who were killed who worked in the Trade Center and also word of some of the brother's family members, some who were firefighters. We all wanted to help, but the problem was we had to wait for orders. See by now the fire department command had pulled together and regrouped. Officers who were chiefs had to step up and take control of the chain of command. It was the first time I had seen the guys since I had gone down to Ground Zero on the eleventh. The two brothers who were with me came up and gave me a hug. It was a bond we all have that we will remember forever. I was standing in the kitchen telling them where I had gone after getting off the rig and walking in the pit on the West Side. The stories were flying around the room varying from running for their lives to seeing victims jumping out windows. The hope for finding survivors alive was not looking good. They were all waiting for orders. I told them I am driving down, and if anyone wanted to come with me, I would take them. This is when the match lit the fuse on the stick of TNT. It was all the tension, frustration, helplessness, hurt, and realizing that it was not just about brothers killed, but now their children! Hearing that brothers were looking for their children, children looking for their fathers and mothers was just too much. One of the lieutenants, who was a firefighter with me told me I could not go down; he said I would have to wait for an order. I told him I was just down there the past two days! He told me he was ordering me not to go because it was firefighters like me that don't think before they do things. That was it! The explosion of emotions came out. I told him I was just down in the hole bagging bodies; Where was he? He said he was down there when building number seven came down, and he was running for his life. I said, "Yea you never made it down into the hole to search?" Some of the brothers sat there and never got up. It was like they were in shock, to see me this mad. I said to the lieutenant, "Let's take this outside!" Brothers got up and tried to calm me down, but it was too late. I already stepped over the line. You see everything from the last year just came to a boil, from the five knee operations, my struggle to get back to full duty, the loss of all the brothers before September 11 and now the helplessness of the past two days was just too much for me to take. I had to help, and nothing was going to stop me except the captain. The captain came in and this was the same captain who told me not to get into the rig down on Duane Street and screamed at me when I got off the rig near the South Tower. He came into the kitchen, and he screamed at everyone to get out except me. He told me he had enough of me running around doing whatever I want and not taking orders. He said, "You told the officer you wanted to take him outside and settle it?" I said, "Captain let me tell you my side of the story." He looked at me and said, "Ok but when you're done talking, you call the medical office and find a job to do and whatever they tell you to do, do it! So I explained the frustration and the loss I was feeling and the helplessness and the need to help. We ended it on a handshake and again he said, "Call the medical leave desk and get a job!" So before I made the call I went over to the officer that lit the fuse, and I apologized and he said to me, "Chris I never thought you felt that way about me." I told him I don't; it just all built up inside of me and it didn't take much to have it come out. He apologized, and we shook hands and hugged. We both understood the frustration we were both were feeling. We both had the loss of great friends. After shaking hands, I was ready to make the call. A captain answers the phone at the medical desk. I tell him the story about my knee and that my captain wanted me to find a light duty job. The captain at the medical office said to me, "Chris, you do what you think you need to do!" I said to him, "I have to get down there and search for the brothers and survivors." He said, "Then that's what you do, God bless you and be safe!" I hung up the phone and knew what I had to do. I packed my gear into the car and headed back to Ground Zero. Out of respect to my captain, I told him I called, and the medical office gave me a job. He said," That's great. Now go do it!" I walked into the kitchen, and all the brothers were around still waiting for an order. They said, "Chris what job did they give you?" I told them the medical desk told me to do what I think I need to do." They all looked at me and shook their heads with a smile and said be safe brother!

40

I Got the Message

Now feeling better about the medical office's message to do what I think I need to do, I felt like I was doing the right thing and that it was not out of disrespect for Captain's orders; I was following my heart. I was loading up my car for the trip to Ground Zero when one of the brothers came over to me and said, "Chris, a few of the brothers took your advice and are driving down, and the Captain went with them." I smiled and knew that I was making the right move. On my way down, I received a call from my son. His girlfriend's neighbor was a chief who was missing after the attack on the Trade Center. I had worked with him and had a lot of respect for him as a fire officer and as a man. He was in Manhattan at the time and off duty.

When the first plane hit the Trade Center, he raced downtown into the towers. My son told me that the chief had called from under the rubble and spoke to one of his children on the phone and told them he was trapped and was running out of air and didn't know where he was. I was in disbelief but in my heart was the word HOPE... this was just what I wanted to hear, but on the other hand, I was helpless not knowing where he was, sixteen acres where do you start? My son told me to be safe, that he loved me and not to do anything stupid or crazy. I thought to myself; *it's too late*. I grabbed a parking spot off of Greenwich Street and started running towards the hole. That adrenaline kicked in when I got the call. I saw a brother from a company in our battalion. I asked him if he heard about the chief calling his family. He told me no, but I know it was a great feeling to think that he was alive. We passed four charter buses full of workers in white hazmat deluxe coveralls with hoods. I asked one of the workers where they were going? He turned and told me they were cleaning out the phone company. I told him it looked like they were cleaning the inside of a building. He

271

agreed! I knew right then and there that what we were getting into was not good for our health or our future, but nothing was going to stop me from doing what I thought was right. I knew that if I were trapped under the wreckage, all the brothers who lost their lives would have been digging for me. I couldn't leave them. We got into the hole and didn't know where to start. I said a silent prayer that no matter where I started digging it would be the right spot. I saw a few brothers that had worked with the chief in the Bronx, and they knew about the call and had an idea just where he might be. It was along the Westside Highway. We started digging where there was a seventy-foot twisted steel beam from the outside structure of the Trade Center. We found a few body parts around it and figured that with the void there may be room for a car trapped where the chief might be, but during the digging, we found a body. It was in the void but buried with debris. So we all took turns going into the void and grabbed dirt and shoveled it out from both ends, till we freed the young man's body. It took hours, during which the thought panicked us that the trapped chief was running out of air. When we got the body out, we pulled him from his shoulders and his bones were broken but his body was kept intact by his suit jacket. His eyes were open. I looked right in his eyes wondering what terror he must have seen as the towers came down. I thought about his loved ones who looked into those same eyes and told him they loved him, or maybe those eyes that seen his children's first smile. I will never forget that young man. I prayed for him and his family. To say how crazy it was down in the hole is an understatement. After one of the brothers had come out of the void to free the young man out, he had a strange look on his face and just wet himself. The night went by with bagging bodies and finding remains of victims. Still all along we were hoping, we would find the chief. The helpless feeling of knowing he could be suffering was heart wrenching. Every time you would hear brothers scream, "Quiet" around the sixteen acres you had hope that they found him, but it was always followed by, "Back to work!" The night seemed to drag, but the hope never left. In the morning word came down by one of the brothers that the phone call home from the chief was an accident. He had never called his home. What had happened was one of the brothers called his house to reassure his family that we were doing everything we could to find him and hung up the phone. Later in the day, he had his phone in his turnout coat, and it hit redial to the chief's home. His son picked it up, and with the same hope that carried me, was the same hope that made him hear his father's voice telling him he was still alive, but the hope came to an end when they declared the chief dead. I took the news badly, but crazy as it may seem to a non-firefighter who would give up on finding survivors, we never gave up. As the days went by and the body count rose, you start to see the search and rescue dogs become recovery dogs. The days went by, and the smell of death was in the air, but I still held on to hope because I've heard stories of people trapped for weeks in earthquakes. I figured some crazy firefighter would find a way, but it was not to be. The days all seemed to roll into one another. The bucket brocades brought some closure to families by bringing their loved ones back to them. I lost track of the days. It didn't mean anything to me. I had that mission in my heart, and that's all I knew.

It was early one morning, some of the brothers found three firefighters in a stairwell that stood about sixty to seventy feet. The only way to get up there was to have ladders tied up to steel beams. I looked at it and thought to myself; I got to get up there. I prayed that the knee would hold up to the stress and started to climb. I would hold on and take a break every new ladder I stepped on. I finally made it to the top. In the back of my mind, I figured no one from my company would see me up here, especially the captain. On the top, there were twenty firefighters, construction workers, welders and other first responders. There was a hole where the stairs once were, and it was about eight feet deep and about ten feet round. There were guys waiting to get into the hole to give guys breaks. I looked around, and now you could see to the lower level and the upper level of the Trade Center. It was a sight I will never forget. Smoke still rising out from the fire deep below the steel. I had a chance to get into the hole, and there I saw a body of a firefighter. All you could see is his left leg and his left hand that was still holding his tool. I realized he didn't feel a thing because he never let it go. I prayed he died instantly. There were Scott air packs around the stairwell some were burned; others had exploded from the pressure of the concrete. There were firefighter helmets, turnout gear laying around the stairwell from brothers that just took their gear off and tried to make it up the stairs to search for victims. You have to remember it's over one hundred flights of stairs. This firefighter's turnout coat had his last name on it. Someone told me he was a lieutenant from a Rescue 1 in Manhattan. Same house of one of the brothers I called on the morning of the eleventh. His body would be found days later. You could only fit eight guys in the stairwell, and I was one of them. There was an old time welder cutting steel to free up the lieutenant's body. He cut the steel, and we then handed it up to the brothers who put it off to the side. It took hours of moving debris, but we freed up his body in the midafternoon. There were riggers from other states that placed a line from the top of the stairwell to the bottom level near the West Side Highway. The members from his rescue company came up and removed his body and placed it on a Stokes rescue stretcher, covered his body with the American flag and placed his helmet on his chest and hooked it up to the rigged line. The whole sixteen acres were silent, as they lowered his body over one hundred feet to a waiting fire truck and ambulance. Everyone had their helmets over their hearts saying a prayer for the ultimate sacrifice this brother had made.

Word came up to the top of the stairwell that it was considered unsafe. We were ordered to come down. I was pissed because I figured there were more bodies on those stairs. I climbed out of the stairs and put my head up to get a breath of fresh air. Still figuring I was safe that no one from my company would see me up there, as my head came out of the hole, I hear someone scream Chrissy!!! I recognize the voice; it was one of the brothers from my house. I looked up, and there were five brothers that had stretched a line hitting pockets of fire from above. I looked, and the officer was the lieutenant that I had got into the argument with a few days before. The brothers were laughing their asses off. They said I look like a beat up groundhog coming out of a hole. They were surprised to see me in a place that they couldn't get. I told the officer not to say anything to the captain. He smiled and reassured me he wouldn't, but asked me what company I was working with? I told him about my talk with a captain from the medical leave desk who told me to do what I think I need to do, and that's why I am up here. We shook hands, and the brothers gave me a hug and handshakes. You could see they were proud of what I was doing. It wasn't just what I could do for the victims and their families, but for the company and them. A short time later we were all pulled off the stairs. They felt the stairs were unsafe. I was frustrated thinking about the possibility of brothers and victims trapped, maybe even alive running out of air, seconds away from breathing their last breath. Why are they pulling us off the stairs? Unsafe? The whole area is unsafe. I started to realize I was getting angry, frustrated, but most of all, I was losing that four letter word that had carried me to this point... hope! For the next week and a half, I was a lost soul. Still all along

278

questioning God. Directing my anger towards God, taking a break in the daytime to go to memorial services and funerals for firefighters, a port authority police officer, civilians, Brother's children, then coming back at night to search, trying to give peace to those families who waited for their loved ones remains to be put to rest... My trips to church slowed up. Only when I was at a funeral.......

I realized every day I questioned my faith. It was both a physical and emotional roller coaster. I was running on empty. I had nobody to tell me to take a break from digging and searching for the victim's remains. I kept in contact with family who asked me to take a break. I just told them I was on a mission. The number of the victims were still adding up and word of different brothers who lost their lives saving others... total strangers, people of different races, color, and creeds. Then, finding out that the victims didn't just stop with firefighters but reached into their families; children, wives, brothers of firefighters who I had worked with lost their brothers, some firefighters and others who worked in the towers. There came a point where I didn't want to know. I didn't want to believe that the 343 heroes who I called brothers, and 23 NYPD officers, and 37 officers of the Port Authority and 2753 innocent victims were gone. One night after attending funerals for two young men, a double funeral for an officer's son and his son-in-law, a young man who I had met when he was just a little kid, a young man who also would come to Christmas parties and company picnics, then another officer whose son was a firefighter, that I seen grow up to follow in his father's footsteps to become a firefighter just like his father, then another son of an officer who I worked with, that I realized all this loss was just too much to handle. The funerals were the moving moment that just tore my heart out. I went back to the hole later that night to continue our search for these young men, other friends, and their family members. I was physically exhausted and mentally drained. My heart cried for these innocent victims of this cowardly act. The hurt was bone deep. The rage and anger grew in my heart for those who committed these terrorist attacks on innocent victims. It was early the next morning when I just took a few minutes to catch my breath. The sun was rising, and I was sitting on a twisted piece of steel next to the West Side Highway. The sky was a beautiful maroon color. I looked around, and seen dump trucks, cranes, welders in buckets cutting steel beams and I realized that there was nothing left for me to do. They were moving debris to other locations and searching through it for remains. I looked up at the sky and asked forgiveness for questioning God and thanked him for a chance to give peace to families looking for their loved ones. I cried my eyes out on that beam. I walked out towards Greenwich Street looking at signs and pictures taped and glued to lamp posts, constructions signs, plywood walls, store windows, some still carrying the white dust with messages written in them like *God Bless America! We will rebuild! Pray for our FDNY and NYPD!* Every step I took towards my car I would look at these faces of missing loved ones and wondered if maybe I had helped along with the others brothers in giving peace to families. Every picture of a missing young man I looked at reminded me of that young man I had looked at in the eyes. His face will never leave my mind...

41

It's All about Respect

Leaving the *Trade Center, Ground Zero, The Hole, the Pit* whichever way you describe it; it was a burial ground for innocent victims just going about their business of making a living for their families. For others it was a resting place for the brave men and women who put their lives on the line to help save thousands of people, mothers, fathers, sisters, brothers, black, white, brown, people from countries that don't really see eye to eye with our ways of life, total strangers. I felt I had a hole in my heart and soul the size of the sixteen acres. I felt and still feel that it's an open wound that will never heal. The pain I felt in my knee was no comparison to the hurt that I felt for all the brothers that were killed and their families, for the fathers that lost sons.

As I walked away, I met a friend who I hadn't seen in years. He was a construction worker. He just drove down to the Trade Center wanting to help. He got in with his union card. You see these are the types of friends you gravitate to being a firefighter; people that when things go really bad, you want them stand beside you. We talked about the old days of football games and softball leagues we had played in, all awhile just touching on things we had just done and seen in the last two and a half weeks. We talked about the brothers I worked with and their losses. When we got to his house, we hugged, and I told him thanks for spending time searching for victims and friends and the brothers we had lost.

I went home for the first time and spent time with family and friends. It was a lost feeling knowing you are leaving unfinished work down at Ground Zero, but it was a weird feeling because for the two and a half weeks of seeing nothing but devastation, it was like a different world a couple of miles away. I had called the firehouse and asked them about upcoming funerals and memorials services. The brother told me they had a list of about twenty-five sheets, some of those were for the children of brothers I worked with. I promised my son Kris I'd have lunch with him, and I needed to spend a day with him because the pain of my friends losing children, makes you realize how short life is and how unpredictable it can be. He had to do a stop off and pick up a deer he had butchered, so I took the trip. When we got to the butcher, a small place privately owned, I walked in with him, and as we passed a pile of deer hooves, it all came rushing back to me, those days spent digging and searching for bodies and only finding human remains. I had to walk away and sit in the car and cry. I didn't realize it then, but years later they would diagnose other brothers and me with PTSD (Posttraumatic stress disorder). My son came back into the car and seen me upset, and I explained to him what had just happened. He gave me a hug. I didn't tell him what I had seen, but I told him that I don't want anyone else ever to have to do or see what we did. After spending time with him, I realized I needed to talk to someone to get help with my feeling of loss and endless nightmares. I had seen my two younger sons and took them fishing up near West Point in a row boat. We had a great time, but I knew I had more work to do. I needed to get the list of the brothers and other victim's funerals and memorial services. I took those two days spent with the kids to reflect on my life and the changes I needed to make. One was to become a better father, a better person, a better firefighter a better Christian, but I still questioned God. I felt as though he left me. He abandoned the brothers that cried out his name in the stairway or the young man running for his life or the countless remains that were someone's loved ones. The families at home that prayed for their loved ones to be safe, but their prayers were not answered. I realized that the knee couldn't take all that pounding of walking in the debris, so my next mission was to start on the funerals full time. I was going to families that I knew and being there for the brothers that lost loved ones, trying to make every firefighter's funeral. I picked up the paper at the firehouse and sat at the kitchen table hearing the story of a brother I worked with that went down from the medical office with another brother and he left a note for his daughter and wife. Afterwards, the two of them ran out and when the south tower came down, he ran one way and the other brother ran the opposite way and my friend, a brother, was killed leaving a note for his young daughter, telling her that he will always love her. Then there was the story of another brother that needed to get out early on September 11 because his wife was having their first child and he had to take her to her doctor's appointment. He had another brother come into work early. He did, and the brother walked to the train and by the time he got home the planes had hit the World Trade Center. Knowing that they would be down there, he called and left a message to his partner. That call was never returned. The brother was killed in the collapse. When his son was born he named him after his partner killed on September 11. Hearing these stories made me start to think...maybe God didn't leave prayers unanswered? Maybe it's just the way things were supposed to be. I started my journey, my new mission. There were days I went by myself, so no one would see me cry. There were days we went as groups, but going by myself I could go to four funerals a day, sometimes five. Going over bridges without paying tolls, the collector would give you a salute and wave you through, knowing you were going to lay a brother to rest. They tried to space out the firefighters because you wanted a good turnout, but sometimes the family wanted things done differently, and their wishes came first. It was not like there was ever a question of brothers not being able to pay their respects to one of our own, but to have so many on one day would be tough for everyone. I remember going to Long Island to a funeral for a captain in the Port Authority. She was the only female captain killed at the Trade Center. I took a mass card that would later give a picture to her face in a place three hundred miles away. There was a firefighter's funeral twenty minutes away from hers. I went to that one; then took a ride to Staten Island for a memorial of another brother. He was the brother of a brother in my firehouse. Then on to Brooklyn for a wake, a closed casket. This went on for weeks and months and years. I averaged about two to three a day. Some people I knew, others I didn't, but I always said to myself that this might have been someone in the group I was digging who we found. That's what drove me to go to so many. The thought that I prayed over that person's remains.

42

Another Door Shuts

I realized that going to funerals and memorial services could be a seven day a week event. I went to some of the memorials, but I felt that going to the funerals was more important. Funerals where families were burying either remains or their loved one's body. During this time, I had called the fire department medical office and told them I had to make up the appointment that was postponed due to September 11. I was on my way back to the greatest job in the world. I still felt that way even, after all, the brothers were killed. It gave me peace to think they were doing what they loved to do which was helping people. I had to get back to work! The need was driven by the brother's deaths. I had a need never to let them be forgotten and not to have all the victims die in vain.

One memorial service I went to was for a Captain, who worked in Manhattan. He was one of the most decorated captains in the history of the FDNY. The memorial service was held in Saint Patrick's Cathedral. The streets were closed down, and there were tower ladders with three ladders extended towards the heavens with a giant American Flag blowing from a gentle breeze. There were over twenty thousand firefighters and police officers and other dignitaries from around the country and the world. We were brought in and seated side by side in the church. It looked like a sea of blue. The eulogy was very emotional. You could see some of the toughest guys wiping tears away from their eyes. This is when the old saying *"Grown men don't cry"* went out the window. We were all hurting. We all walked out to line up for our final goodbye to the Captain not knowing a few weeks later his body would be pulled from the wreckage, and they would have a funeral to give his family peace knowing we brought him home.

The pain didn't just exist with the fire department. It went further. There was a head writer and other casting people from the Conan O'Brien show who had called me during the attack to make sure I was ok. They were extremely upset. I called them up and reassured them I was ok, and they asked me if I could stop by and see them. I told them I would, and after the captain's memorial, I went over to Rockefeller Center. I had a few of the brothers with me, and we went up to see them. They came out and greeted me with hugs and handshakes and well wishes. I was talking to them in the hallway. It started with a few of them listening, to a group of them, and finally Conan came out and shook my hand and asked me if I was alright, and if I needed anything or if the brothers needed anything. I told them we need your prayers. I told them to pray for the families of the dead. They asked me what they could do. How do we go back to work making people laugh? I told them we need you to put smiles on people's faces again. It's going to be tough, but we need normalcy. We left with hugs and handshakes. One of them came out and gave us Conan O'Brien rain jackets. These are the special people I called friends. Another friend called me and asked if I would come down to the AFTRA (American Federation of Television and Radio). Being I was a member of AFTRA and being a union member down at the Trade Center, it was an honor for me to address a large group of people and to pass my message on to them that *we must never forget* the brave men and women who lost their lives saving others. I also remember telling them about grown men crying. This was part of my drive to get back and pass the message on and my new mission! Keep the brothers alive in my heart.

I went to the fire department doctor. The doctor was glad to see that I was ok. The doctor asked me if I had been down there and I asked her what she thought. She said she hoped I was careful. I told her I was. She explained to me what I needed to do to get back to work. I had eight screws and two metal plates on both sides of my knee holding it together. I needed to get the metal removed before I could get back to work. I gave her a hug and told her thanks for helping me. She told me to be back in a week. I called my orthopedic and made an appointment. I had to have X-rays of the knee and bring them to his office. After looking at them, he said the bone is healed and that he could remove the screws and plates with confidence! I thanked him. He said this hasn't been an easy road for you. I told him I am on my way back. He said, "You firefighters really love your job!" I said, "Doc it's a way of life; a love that I cannot explain." He smiled and said he could see that. I left his office and headed to Saint Lucy's to ask for forgiveness on doubting God's plans. I went there and sat on the bench overlooking people coming in to be blessed by the holy water. They all came in with bottles and filled them up. I wondered to myself if their prayers were being answered. I would find out about my prayers being answered in a week when I got the metal taken out of my knee. The door has been opened.

I've been waiting for almost a year and the day has finally arrived. A year of operations, loss and disappointment and now I will be able to get back to the greatest job in the world, the New York City Fire Department! I get to the hospital, and the nurses know me by my first name by now. After two operations and the two and a half week stay, it was like my home away from home. I am prepped and ready to go. They wheel me into the operating room, and I say to myself that this is it! The feeling of relief, happiness, pride, and the next and last step to get back and make a difference in the firehouse, all for the memories of the brothers we lost before and on September 11, 2001. The doctor comes over and says, "This is it! You are on your way back!" The anesthesiologist comes in, and the next thing I know is I am in the recovery room. I see the nurse coming in and checking my EKG and other vital signs. I try to get a grip on what's going on, but I am still in la la land. As I start coming out of it, a nurse walks in and checks my pulse. She turns to me and asks," Mr. Edwards, "Have you ever had a heart problem?" I joke with her and say, "Well the brothers in the firehouse say I don't have a heart." I looked at her, and she didn't smile. She gave a grin with a slight nod of the head like to say that's funny, but I have something serious to tell you. I said, "No, why? Is there something wrong? Like what else could go wrong. She said they found something wrong on the EKG and that I should see a cardiologist. I was like, "Are you kidding me?" She said, "No it might be serious." I told her I would when I get home. The thought of a heart problem would never have entered my mind. I was in great shape if it wasn't for my knee. I left the hospital with a bittersweet feeling in my stomach. I didn't tell any of my family or friends what the nurse said. I was going back to work, one way or another! The next day I went over to Saint Lucy's and prayed. I asked God how this could this be. I have done everything I was supposed to do. I have prayed, gone to church, even stopping in on weekdays. How could you do this to me?!! I didn't care about no heart problem. My hope was fading, and my faith was tested again and again. I was going back to the firehouse one way or another. The five operations I went through just tested my faith, hope and love and I came out of it with a heart problem. No way was I going to tell the FD doctor what that nurse said. I was opening the final door to a long, physical and emotional journey to get back to the FD. I go in to see the FD doctor he looks at my chart and says you went through a real tough time. I told him yes, but it will all be worth it when I get back to the firehouse. He smiled and looked at the x-rays of the before and after. He says, "What I am going to do is put you on light duty till all the holes heal in the bone." He counts out loud 1, 2, 3, 4, 5, 6, 7 and 8 screw holes." He told me in the same breath that I had been through a lot. I just shook my head. I asked him how long would the light duty job be? He told me about four months. Great, four months away. I am back!!! Still knowing what the nurse told me in the recovery room about my heart. The doctor asks me, "Were you down at the Trade center?" I told him, "Yes." He tells me that they were giving WTC medical to all members that were first responders and that I should go in and take the medical, because this was the last week they were giving it. I thought I had nothing to lose. I told him I would. They had a whole medical set up from a breathing test to blood work, to monitoring you for PTSD and depression. Then there was the EKG and blood pressure. I went back in with the results from the testing. He looked at the records and said, "Chris I cannot send you back to work, you have a heart problem. It's called a left bundle branch block. I am going to have to retire you. I couldn't believe what he was saying.

"Doc, I have no heart problem!" He said, "It's right here on the EKG. In my mind, I am saying to myself that this is the second person to tell me about my heart, but I still didn't want to believe him. He said when the EKG reads something on the left side it's a problem when it's on the right side not so bad. Well, when I took the test. The pads were not sticking on my chest because of my hair and they let me take it again and this time, I told them I will shave. He said, "It will come out the same again." I wanted to take it again. He said, "OK." This time, I shaved my chest and came back in with the results. He looked at me and said," I know you really want to come back, but you have a heart problem. I cannot let you go back to work. This is the end of the line. We (FDNY) are going to find out what is wrong with your heart, and then retire you with your knee. I couldn't believe my ears. It was over, my life as a New York City Firefighter has come to an end. The fight, the time spent in hospitals, five operations the pain! For what? Now it's gone. My chances of coming back are over. Bang!! The door is slammed in my face. All the emotions came rushing to my heart and head all at once I started to cry. I walked out of the office and wondered what I did wrong to deserve this. I couldn't figure it out. I drove to the firehouse and told the brothers and the officer the bad news, and they were all in shock. Guys couldn't believe it. Everything I went through for nothing. A lot of hugs and tears. Guys were worried about their health conditions and what if they might suffer the same faith as I did with being at the Trade Center breathing in all the fumes and dust. One of the brothers tells me what the FDNY doctors told him. That if you were down at the Trade Center within the first 24 hours or excess of thirty days you could lose anywhere from ten to fifteen years off your life. Then I remember standing in the pile with that smoke rising from burning rubble, deep under the steel, breathing in all the smoke thinking that I was losing years off my life, but all along saying to myself that I would do it all over again. I wouldn't do anything different. The next few weeks the FDNY set up a test to find out what the problem was with the heart. The tests were given at Saint Francis Hospital. The doctors down there said my heart was working at twenty-one percent. He told me I should be on oxygen and in a wheelchair. I shouldn't be able to walk a city block without oxygen. I told him that I felt great. I told him about a bike ride I took from my firehouse in the Bronx through Washington Heights to the West Side Highway to the Trade Center and back up the FDR drive to the William Avenue Bridge, up Third Avenue making the sign of the cross at the job where the burnt bodies were that we bagged years ago, to the Grand Concourse and back to the firehouse. A twenty-eight mile ride, and only stopped once to watch guys on lunch break playing football in the park near Twenty- Third Street. The cardiologist was surprised to see me in great shape with a heart so weak. He asked me if I was at the Trade Center for a period of time and I told him, "*Yes.*" He feels that a lot more firefighters and other first responders will become ill due to the toxic fumes and dust we breathed in. It was a tough time in my life. I was never a quitter, always a fighter, but now throughout the past year of ups and downs and doors closing. I had hit rock bottom as a firefighter and in my relationship. During the next few years, I felt as though I had no identity. The job was letting me go. My relationship was over. My sons were living with their mother. I was lost, but instead of keeping my faith, hope, and love for God, I pulled away from church and God. I was looking for answers in books and others faiths, but never getting the answers I wanted to hear. Why God? Why close all these doors? In my mind, it was something I had done wrong. I still had in a far back part of my mind the thought that the FDNY would take me back, and it would all work out, but during the weeks following the heart doctor's report, I got custody of my sons from their mother. It was something that was not planned. It was something that just came out of nowhere. I went to get an order of protection against her, and the judge asked me questions that had to do with my boys. I told them the truth, and the judge awarded me temporary custody. Now the chance of getting back to the firehouse was out of the question. I had my two young sons that I had to raise. The fire department retired me on 6/1/2002. A day that haunted me for years, till my youngest daughter was born on that day four years later. The following year was full of court appearances and lawyers and doctors' appointments. The final outcome was I got custody of my sons. I had a new mission in my life and that was to be there for my children and a full-time father.

43

Footprints in the Sand

I needed a place to raise my sons and went to look at two foreclosures in a town called Warwick, NY. I didn't have the money, but I figured it was a shot and a move in the right direction. We took a look at two townhouses and after meeting the neighbors, I knew this was the right place to start my new beginnings for my family. After putting a bid in, I got a call back from the salesman, and he said they accepted the offer. This was a sign of things to come. Not looking at it as a message from God, because I was still upset about the past year and a half. I had started my new mission in life. It was not without bumps and bruises along the way. My son had a new school, but my other son decided I was too strict and went back with his mother. I figured if my heart were going to be tested, it would have been in the first two years of settling in. Between court appearances and doctors' visits, I was on the run every day. I had to go back to court, and it cost me over thirty thousand dollars. The money I didn't have, but in a strange way it all worked out. Going through it was hell. I was being abused by the lawyers when I went into court, but I came out with the prize, my son!

All during this time, I was not looking to my right or left. I felt like God had abandoned me. I was always questioning why things were so difficult. Everything was going as good as could be, but I could not see it. My girlfriend moved in a year after the FDNY said I couldn't perform active fire department duties. My second daughter was born. All during this time, my body started to break down. I had problems with my shoulders and had to get it totally replaced only a month before my daughter was born. I still was not seeing the wonderful things going on around me because the bad and the troubled times were still swirling inside my mind. I had bought a house in Lake of the Ozark,

Missouri because I had family that lived out West. They decided to move out there years ago. I figured I would someday move there. It was a beautiful house on the lake. I loved to fish there. I had to sell it because I couldn't afford the two houses and the lawyer's fee. I was struggling to keep my head above water. My son and I drove out there to pick up all the furniture from the house and bring it to the new house. Well, it was right at this time that the story of the Mosaic which I told you about happened. The Mosaic story was meant to be by the power of God and the brothers and friends I had lost. It was a million in one chance that my friend stopped into the same school and bought this flag for the brothers and me. I had good twenty-two hours to think of that and the message and the gift that God had just made happen. I called my friend and his wife to tell them what I had just found out, and they remembered speaking to a woman and answering her questions about where the flag would be hung. We all agreed that God and the brothers had a lot to do with it! This is the messages that confused me because on one hand good things could happen and on the other hand, so could bad. These were the messages I would fight within my head. Never really getting an answer till later when I took off my blinders and seen the messages. The Mosaic proudly hangs in the firehouse in the Bronx surrounded by the pictures of the brave heroes I call my brothers!

We lived in the townhouse for three years and final sold it for a lot more than what I paid for it. I wanted to get up in the mountains away from people. I loved my neighbors in Warwick. My son was doing well in school and with wrestling and all sports, but I needed to find a place where I could find peace within myself. I had nightmares almost every night. Nightmares of being chased and fighting people in black clothes with grease covering their bodies. I would fight them, and they would stop moving. Then as I walked away, the chase continued, running down dark allies. I would wake up just to stop the nightmare, but when I would try and sleep again they were back. Then there were dreams of being in the hole with bodies that were torn apart and the people telling me to help them. An arm would grab me; it would tell me to find the rest of its body. Another dream I had was being in the firehouse and getting a run and looking all over for my turnout coat and helmet. The firetruck ended up leaving me behind as I was chasing it. These dreams were happening all the time! Even today I get these dreams. I had to find a peaceful place, so I headed to the mountains of a small town called Sparrowbush, New York alongside the Delaware River about forty miles west from where I was living. I went up one day and looked at some property. One of the brothers lived down the road. The house was being built and the builder said if I want it, it's mine and shook my hand. I explained to him about selling my other house first. He said that was no problem; it's yours. Wow, one day and I find a place! I started to think of all the messages that were being sent my way by God or the brothers? Maybe this was going to be the place I would get my answers and find some kind of peace, but I had to think of my family and put their needs first. The school had a great reputation for football and wrestling. Two Olympian wrestlers came from the town. Pure blue collar town made up of hard working people with over sixteen religious houses of worship. My son excelled in school and sports. During this time, I had a total of three total joint replacements and weeks in and out of the hospital with heart issues to breathing problems. I know my time is limited. I always remember what the doctors told us about the first twenty-four hours to the over thirty hours, losing anywhere from ten to fifteen years off your life. That's when I realized I needed God more than ever. I found my father's mass card, and I read it. It was called *Footprints in the Sand*. It told the story about how there was only one set of footprints in the sand, and the person questioned God why when I needed you the most you were not with me, through the toughest times of my life, I was alone! God turned to the person and said, "That's when I carried you." I thought about it and reflected on my life and said that's it. From every operation, that failed, to the troubled relationships, to the deaths of all the brothers. During the pain of all the loss, the disappointment of not going back to the firehouse and the stress of the court appearances, you were right by my side, and I didn't see your messages. I remembered that last day down at the Trade Center and sitting on that twisted steel beam and crying because I was alone and helpless, just like the footprints in the sand. I wanted to thank God, but I wasn't too sure how, so I found a church in the town, a Catholic Church. I would drive my son to school and get to church at nine o'clock. This started out a day here and a day there. Then I started going every day. This went on for three years, everyday same time 9 am to 9:30 am. I felt pain and loss and the hurt when I walked in, but when I left it was like a weight had been lifted off my chest. I would walk in and put my finger in the holy water, make the sign of the cross, just like I had done for years at Saint Lucy's and all the other churches along my way. I would walk all the way to the left and count seven pews up, and that's where I sat every day Monday thru Friday and Sunday. I still had a few questions I wanted answered so after mass I would drive up to the top of this mountain and ask you questions, like why? Why? Why? Then one day you gave me the answer. *Take off your blinders and look around you Chris. Don't just look at the sad times the*

hurtful and painful times. Look at your gifts...
Your children, your family, your job, and the
people you have met along the way. The good
that taught you, the bad that gave you pain, but
to feel the pain was a lesson, to feel the loss of
loved ones means they loved you back. You miss
the physical touch of your brothers but their
smiles, and their laughs will be with your
forever. Your work is not done yet. This is why I
asked you all these questions because I felt lost,
but I looked at the prints through my life and
realized I needed someone to carry me. I am
writing this story not for me, but for my children
and grandchildren who may never get to know
who or what I was about. To them I say... *You*
will hear stories from your mothers and fathers
that might add more life to me then I really had,
but I want you all to know I loved you all very
much and will always be around you. I have
made plenty of mistakes along the way never
really meaning to hurt anyone's feelings or
emotions, but I leave for you my tracks in the
sand!

I feel like I have more to give so I have joined a
Disaster Assistance Response Team with the

FDNY and the Red Cross. I have a thirst that cannot be quenched to keep my brothers alive wherever I go throughout the country. Giving back to the same people who on that terrible day on September 11, 2001, got down on their hands and knees and prayed for us. I feel the need to thank every one of them because those prayers carried me through those horrible days for our city and our country and the FDNY and all the first responders who were murdered that day. Maybe I can sit down and write about the payback I owe all of you who read this book. May God bless you and the FDNY and all the victims of September 11, 2001, and all the others who have died since. Thank you, Linda Lucas (Cotter) for giving me
the inspiration to write this story for my children's memories of their old man!!

Coming Through the Flames Poem Inspired by the Book....
By...Linda Lucas

I sit on this mountain looking back at my past.
The blinders are off and I see all "at last."
Becoming a firefighter and dancing with the red devil
As I **Come Through the Flames** my heart is now level.

I've come to know that people can change.
My perspective on life has changed on this day.
I've made mistakes and finally can say
That all things make sense when we learn how to pray.
To go through hard times is like fighting a fire.
Coming through the Flames and safety for all
Your ultimate desire.

During the saddest times in my life when friends
Were lost to an unspeakable evil.
I've learned to cherish their memories and know
Not everything is foreseeable.
I pray to the heavens and remember them with love.
Coming Through the Flames and seeing angels from above.

We never can take for granted the small memories of each day.
The people we love and signs in our way.
I can only say from this point onward.
Regrets are the past, it's time to look forward.
To the gift we are given of life in each day.
The heat of the fire is a fear that is givin.
Coming Through the Flames a metaphor for livin.

The Blinders are off as I look for the signs.
The lessons I learned and knowledge through time.
I know I'm protected as I seek to protect
My guardian angels give me direction and
Never let me Neglect.
I tell those I love that your life will be blessed
Your **Come Through the Flames** as the signs will suggest.

I pray on this mountain as I look to the clouds.
It's taken me awhile to say this out loud.
That my children are angels who make me feel proud.
Coming Through the Flames has taught me to never be sad
The best gift I've gotten was to be called your dad.

312

A Locker Full of Memories

- Special thank you to Matthew Daly for letting me use his pictures.

Brothers of E81

Keeping it Light

Team Work

We work as a team and play as a team

317

OH NO....
NOT AGAIN!

BUSTED

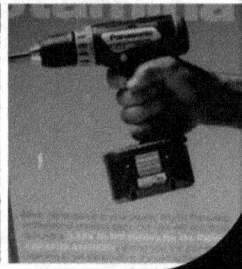

Other Careers.. long story..

318

Giving Back

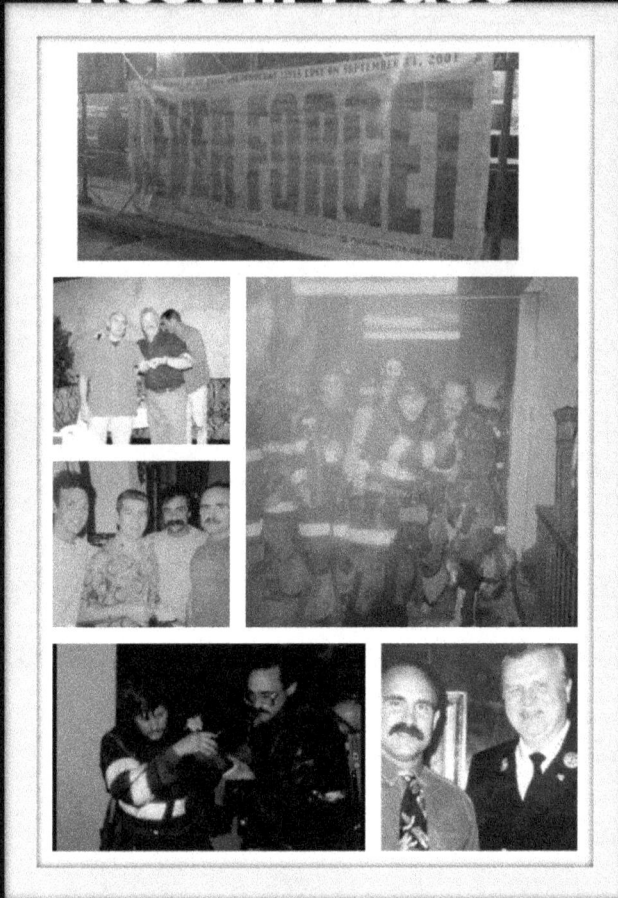

Never forget the brothers that paid the ultimate sacrifice before and after September 11, 2001.

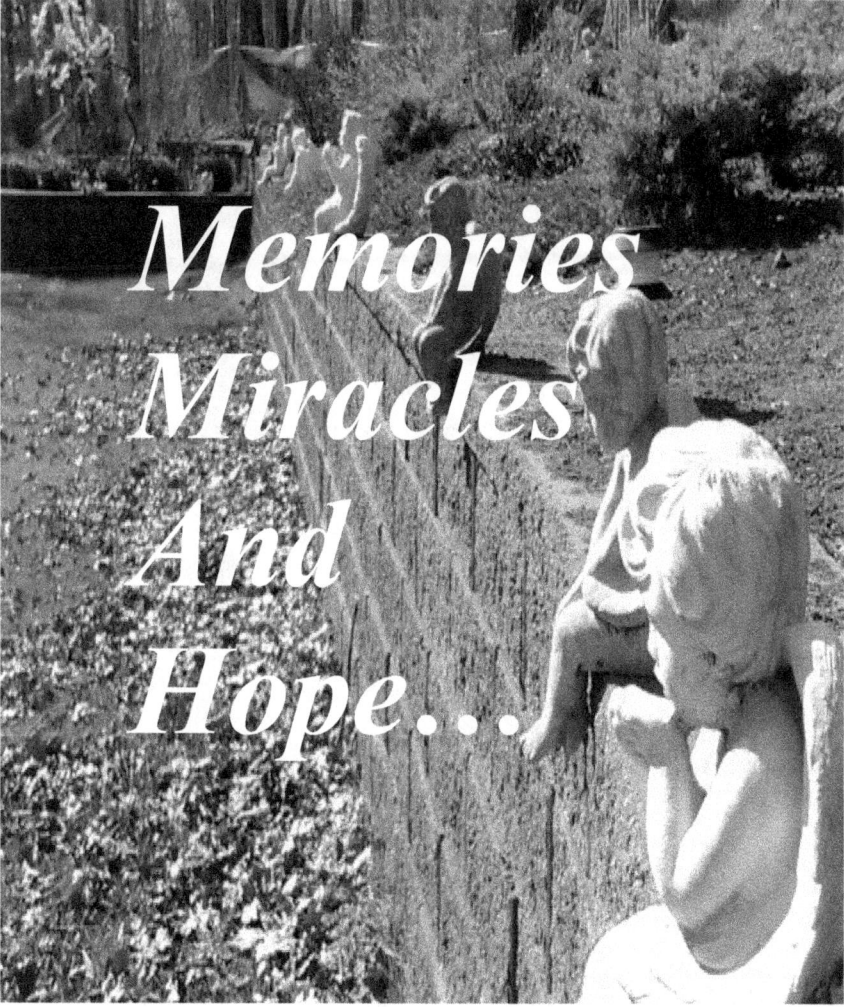

Memories
Miracles
And
Hope...

The Mosaic – Chapter 23

My Baptism, The two alter boys in my baptism.... one was my brother, who my father cut out of the pictures to the left... The one on the right would become my Captain 35 years later in Engine 42 ... Captain I is one of the Greatest officers I, worked for. Never knew he was friends with my brother till we spoke about my Uncle Downtown Larry Brown passing away. I called my Brother and the two of them spoke about old-times...over thirty-five years... people come in and out of our lives. You just have to have your blinders off to see why

A Sign from Above

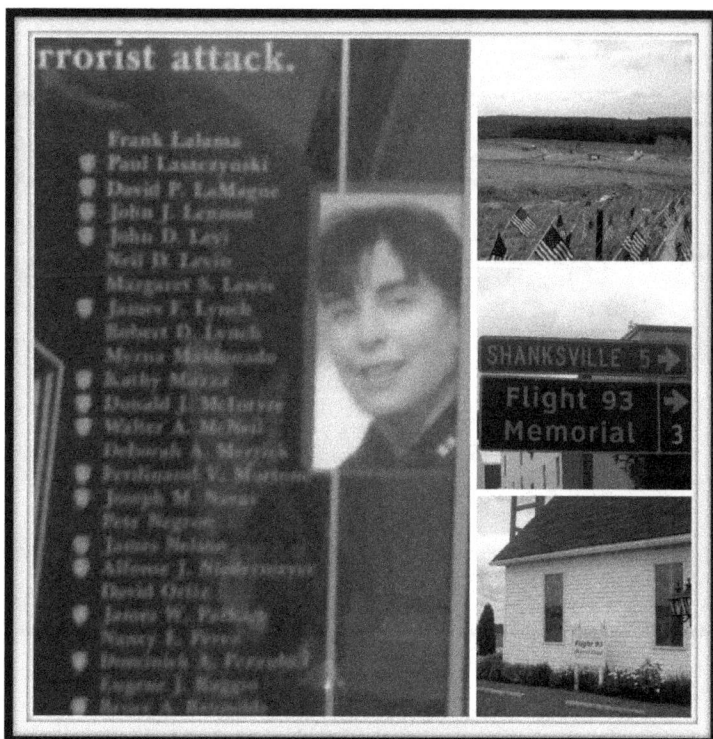

Top... I went to this chapel that is made into a memorial for
victims of Flight 93. I saw this poster for the Port Authority
Police Officers. After September 11, funerals followed and I
went to Kathy Mazza's Memorial service and I had her mass
card on me. When I went to this chapel, I seen her name on
the memorial poster and put her mass card there. I have
held onto that mass card for 10 years. Her name has a face
now so people who stop by Flight 93 Chapel can stop and
say a prayer for her. God Bless all the victims of September
11!
Top Right Corner... Actual crash site of Flight 93
Middle... sign leading to the Memorial
Bottom... Actual chapel

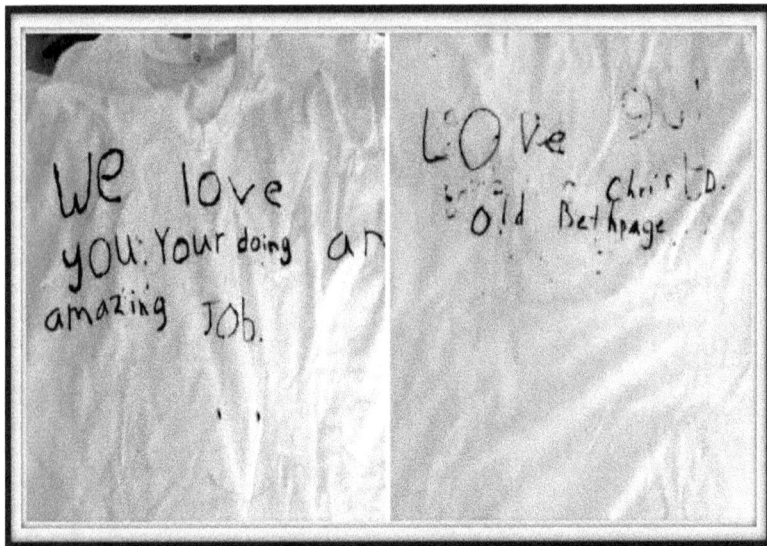

One day at the trade Center on September 11,2001, I was just walking back into the pile when a police officer (white shirt) came over to me and told me about his son in elementary school, that his class made up tee shirts and wanted to give it to a Hero Firefighter, I told his that I was no hero the real heroes are the Brothers who didn't come back. I told him I would be honored to have it but I couldn't wear it. I went home and put that shirt in a clear plastic bag and never wore it....... it's been 15 years!

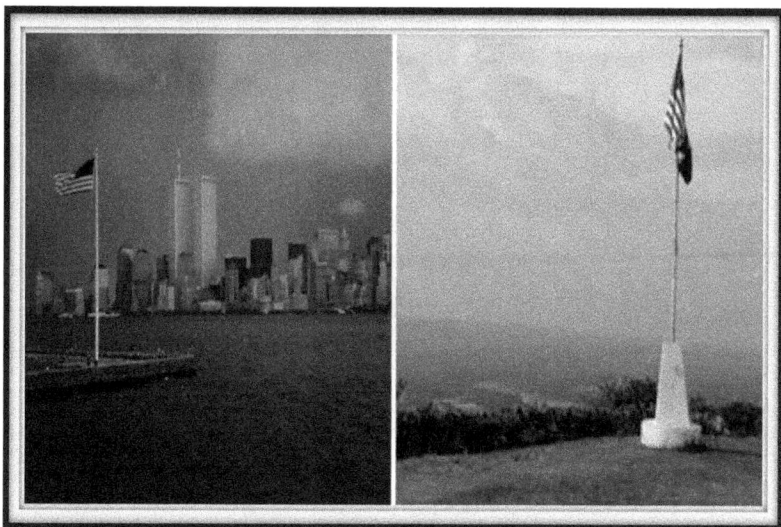

Right... September 10, 2001   Never forget!
Left... the hill where I pray and wrote this book

Family Memories

What it's all about!

Where It All Began...

The Wrecking Crew

Daddy's Girls

Da Boys

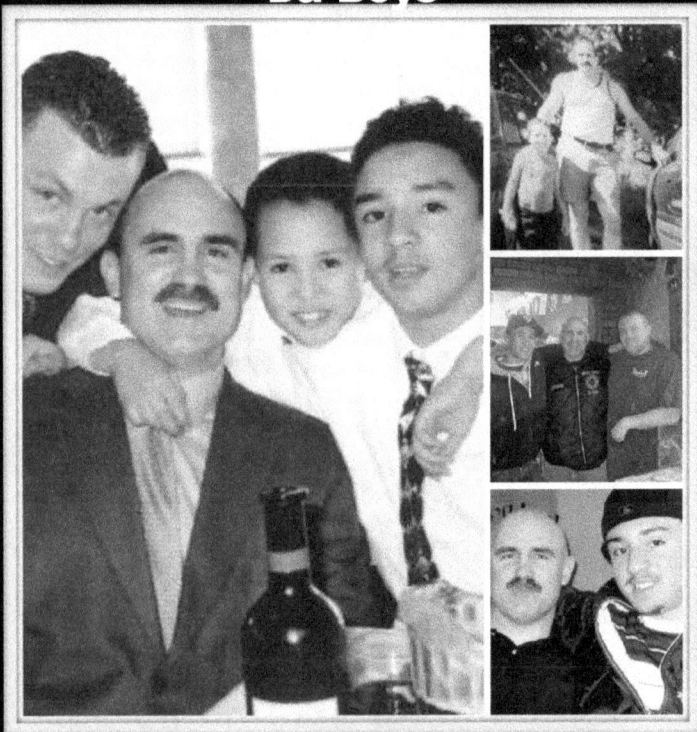

My Hero My Brother the Vietnam Vet

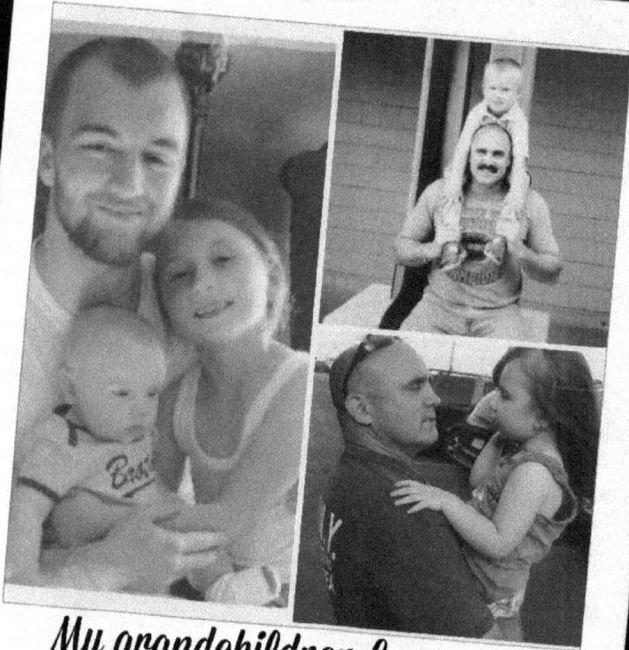

My grandchildren from my daughter Tara

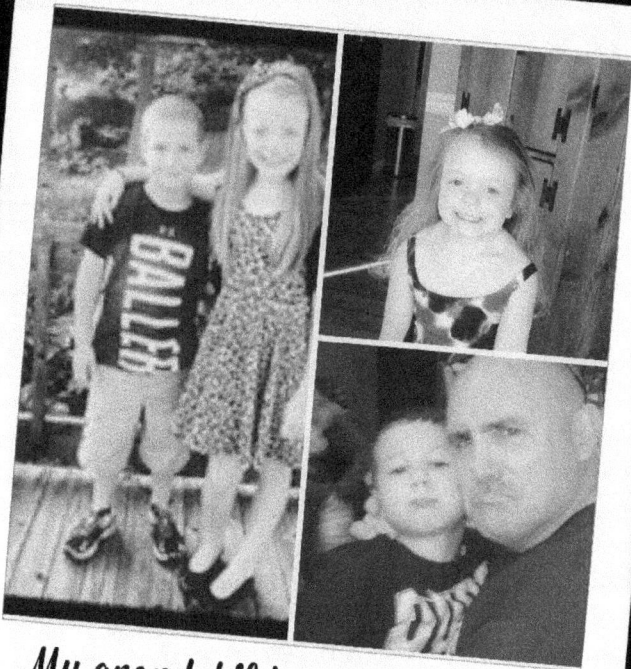

My grandchildren from my son Kris..

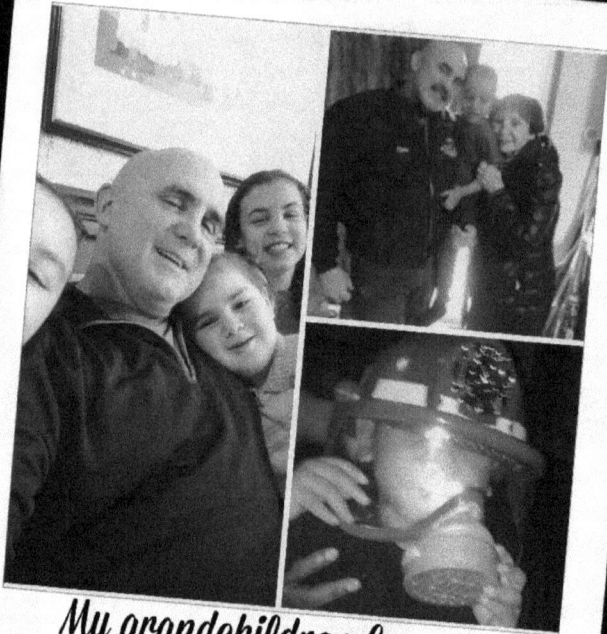

My grandchildren from my son Clint..

Sharing special moments

Passing the torch

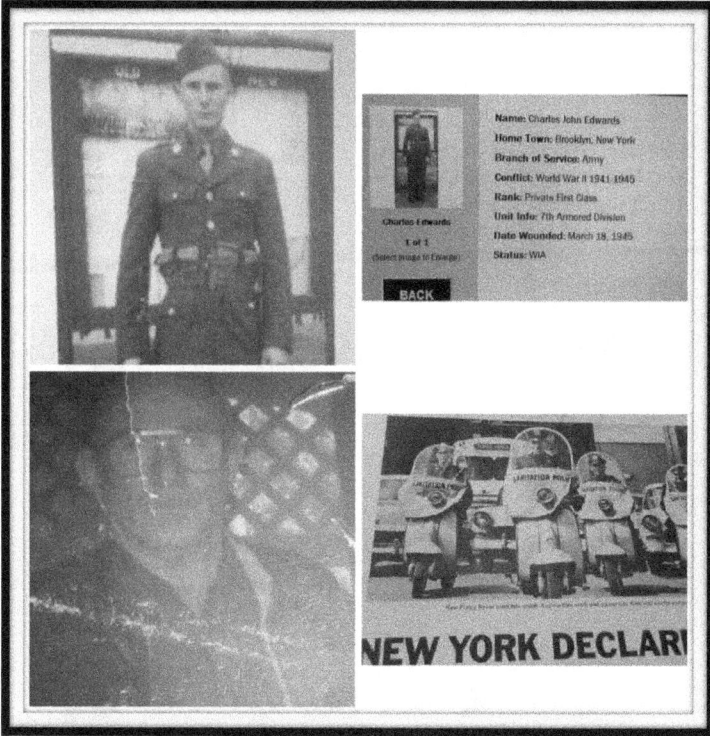

A great man, a great husband, a great father…
My hero, My Father

Downtown Larry Brown… my uncle who died of Lou Gehrig's disease

My good friend Peter Baird with his children Courtney and Peter Jr. and my children Travis and Paige

High School Brothers

High School Friends...

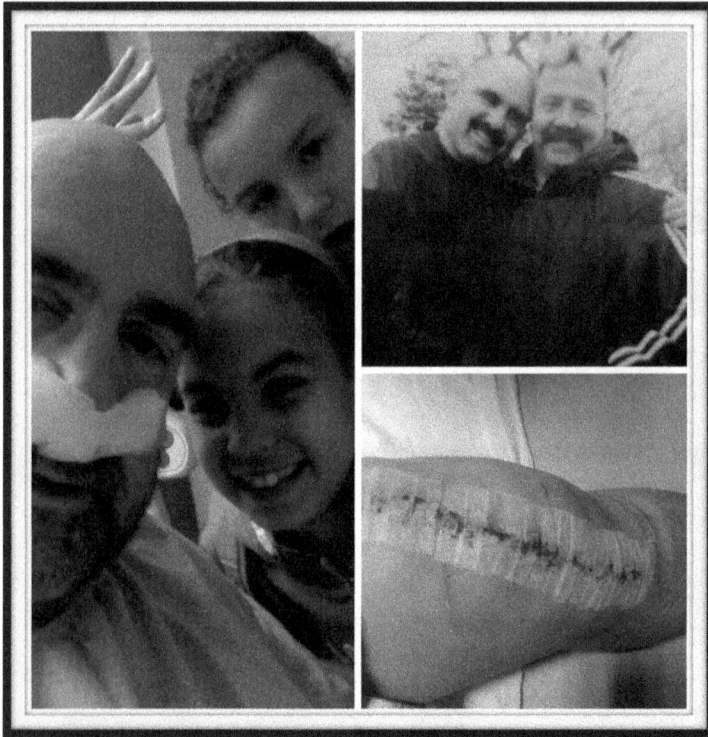

3 out of the 11 surgeries in the past 14 years

The Hulk given to me by my son Travis when he was about 4 years old. The Hulk went through hell and back!

Café Al Mercato in the Arthur Avenue Market in the Bronx, NY

My Blinders are off… Linda Lucas
Upon working on this book with Chris, I've gotten a
few signs. The top left was a picture I took of Chris's
Freedom Tower. When I printed it out what looked to
me like angel wings appeared on top. On the left is a
bear given to me by my Aunt. She had given me a
bunch of things for my new home in a bag. I happened
to stop by the cemetery after she gave me the bag. I
went there to visit my dad's grave which is right near
the fireman's graves from Washingtonville who died on
9/11. I just happened to be thinking of them and
opened the bag and saw this bear who plays "Proud to
be an American" by Lee Greenwood. I've always
associated this song with the loss on that day. It was
my feeling this was meant as a sign… blinders off…
they are still with us.

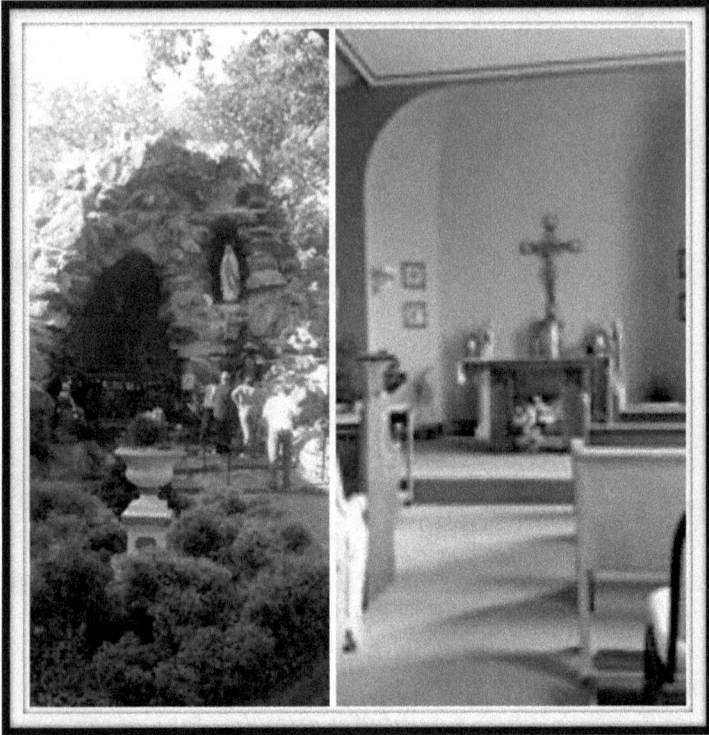

Our Lady of Lourdes, St. Lucy's Grotto in the Bronx and St. Mary's Chapel, Port Jervis

The journey continues to satisfy a thirst that cannot be quenched to help others...Rest in peace my brother Mike Mondello (sitting on the far right)
Rest in peace my brother Louie Fragoso (six from the left in the front row bottom picture)

www.ingramcontent.com/pod-product-compliance
Lightning Source LLC
Chambersburg PA
CBHW052029090426
42739CB00010B/1838